STORES OF THE YEAR/5

STORES OF THE YEAR/5

EDITED BY MARTIN M. PEGLER

RETAIL REPORTING CORPORATION, NEW YORK

Copyright © 1989 by Retail Reporting Corporation

All rights reserved. No part of this book may be reproduced
in any form, by mimeograph or any other means,
without permission in writing from the publisher.

Retail Reporting Corporation
101 Fifth Avenue
New York, NY 10003

Distributors to the trade in the United States and Canada:
Van Nostrand Reinhold
115 Fifth Avenue
New York, NY 10003

Distributed outside of the United States and Canada:
Hearst Books International
105 Madison Avenue
New York, NY 10016

Library of Congress Cataloging in Publication Data:
Main Entry under the title: Stores of the Year/5

Printed and Bound in Hong Kong
ISBN 0-934590-31-1

Designed by Michael Shroyer

CONTENTS

INTRODUCTION

In selecting our Stores of the Year — we used several criteria. Some of our selections are award winners; designs that have been recognized by specialists in the field like the Institute of Store Planners (ISP), Chain Store Age, and by the trade press and the designer's peers. Others were selected because, "un-awarded" and relatively unknown, they are not only successful designs, they are also distinctive and memorable. These qualities — together — make the store easy to recognize, and often entice the shopper to return.

More than ever we are seeing the Cloning Syndrome taking over in malls, in strip centers and on Main Streets. Some retailer's great and novel idea gets picked up, — and sometimes with little change or any respect for the original's concept — it is knocked off — and knocked off again and again. Soon, the creative "original store" is lost in the mire of second rate reproductions. Too often we read in trade publications about the confusion of the shopper in the mall; not being able to find her way back to a store she had previously been in because — "they all look the same." We are finding that some of the "creative originals," — the previously mentioned knocked-off stores, are now rethinking, — revamping and redesigning their operations, and in this volume we are pleased to present some of these "new looks." These are the new, more easily recognized and remembered prototypes. We have attempted to point out what makes each of our selected store designs unique; whether it be the architectural quality, — the decorative theme or devices, — the color scheme, — choice of materials, — lighting techniques, — or the ambience that is created that makes the shopper want to stay.

For the viewer's convenience, we have divided our book into eight broad categories, and within each we have sought to reproduce the stores and shops that give the full fashion spectrum, — that go from one extreme to the other, — from super elegant, super chic to popular priced appeal or even fun and funky. Though some of our selections are "designer boutiques," we are not doing a "snob" book. The reader will recognize some excellent examples of mall stores that may have a broader appeal where price does matter. Some of our selections are targeted for clients "thirty-something" — and over, while others are for those in their teens into the twenties. In this wide range the reader should get a panoramic view of what Women's Specialty Stores, Menswear Shops, and Home Fashions, as examples, are all about in design — in look — in merchandising concepts, — fixturing and lighting as we enter into the last decade of the twentieth century. Some of our selections are avant garde, ultra-new, architecturally advanced into the next century. Others delight in the decorative details and motifs that enhanced the environments of the 18th and 19th centuries. While some stores are slick and sophisticated in silvery metals, floating glass stairways, concrete used with style, and lighting creating un-earthly effects, — others are warm and secure with hand rubbed woods, marble, crystal and brass, and all the other fine materials and textures we immediately associate with "elegant." Some stores are reaching for tomorrow while others coddle their clients in the rich ambience of times gone by — but not forgotten. Both approaches work. It depends upon the client.

In all instances, the stores have a focus. They are designed for a specific retailer, — for a specific client/ shopper, for the showing and selling of a particular type of merchandise. They are designed to leave an imprint on the shopper's mind so that she or he will return again and again. Thus, Stores of the Year / 5 is dedicated to Stores of Distinction; to stores that are unique, — apart, — special, which enhance the merchandise within and send out messages to those without, about the retailer's Fashion Image. In as many cases as possible we have attempted to provide the all-important "Opening Statements," — the store fronts or facades that introduce what lies beyond. Also, for the readers' convenience, — we have reproduced, where available, schematic floor plans or diagrams to help "set the space" and permit the reader to follow the traffic patterns established by the architects/designers. We hope you find our selections interesting, — intriguing — and maybe even inspirational.

Martin M. Pegler, S.V.M.

WOMEN

The concept of Women's Fashions is a many-splendored thing. It is as multifaceted as a finely cut diamond, and as each surface of the diamond reflects light from a different angle, so does each specialty store reflect a woman's different angle, attitude, look, life-style and fashion image. In the past few years we have heard more and more of "specialization," — of "nichemanship," — of finding that special spot in the market that is right for a very special type of shopper, and the Women's Specialty Stores that we have assembled for this chapter suggest the wide market open to fashion shoppers and their changing attitudes.

Women come in all shapes, sizes and ages, — from all strata of society, — with assorted levels of financial security and spending capabilities. There are those who can afford the most expensive and will buy only designer creations in exclusive shops, and then there are those who also know exactly what they want to look like and want to find that fashion image in a price range they can afford. There are, necessarily, degrees of selection and service, — of comfort and convenience, — of pampering and promotion. Our selected shops have each targeted their design toward a particular segment of women shoppers and the stores have been laid out, decorated and dressed to appeal to those customers; to an age group, — to a spending level, — to a life-style, — to a fashion image. The use of space, the degree and type of lighting, the depth of selection and the mass of merchandise presentation, the colors and textures, the building and facing materials, the details and deocrations, the use of and the type of mannequin for form, the display techniques, — all together, like letters in an alphabet, can be rearranged or reorganized to spell out visually what the store is, — and who that store caters to, and why the shopper should enter the store.

The following selections come from all across the United States, from Canada, England and even Brazil. There are "designer boutiques" found on fine shopping streets, and there are "specialty chains" that appear in malls all over the land. Some shops are sumptuous and saturated in marble, crystal and period furniture, while others are crisp, clean and totally contemporary. The lighting may be low-keyed, subtle and "residential" or it may be sparkling, scintillating and very up-beat, — even underscored with colored neon "exclamation marks." In every case the "picture" presented is complete; fixtures, furniture and furnishings are integrated into a design that expresses the Retailer's image and calls out to the desired shopper.

From super-sophisticated, super-elegant, "designer" and "exclusive" — to "up-scale" — to "popular priced," a store can and should be attractive and effective, — should be convenient and comfortable, and provide what the shopper expects. It should leave an impression, one that the customer takes with her along with her purchase, — one that brings her back to the shop over and over again.

Left: Joseph's, London, England

JOSEPH'S

Fulham Rd., London, England

Designer:
EVA JIRICNA ARCHITECTS
Design Team:
EVA JIRICNA / JON TOLLIT

Structural Engineer:
WHILBY & BIRD, LONDON
Shopfitters:
QUICKWOOD, LTD., LONDON

The site of approximately 1000 meters sq., on two levels, is in the now highly fashionable Brompton Cross area. This is a mini-department store that includes a variety of departments including women's wear, accessories and furniture. Working with the "awkward geometry" of the site, the designer had to "create order and focus whilst maximizing the retail space and provide sufficient fitting rooms and stock areas." A

central axis was formed onto which the staircase was relocated, — and the axis culminated in a full height mirror on the realigned back wall.

Spanish marble is used on the floor and white plaster, sealed with bees wax, coats the walls. Woodwork is cherrywood with a diluted black stain and clear lacquer. Black was used only to clarify and accentuate.

ANNA BASSETT'S CLAIRE PEARONE

Design:
JON GREENBERG
ASSOCIATES, BERKLEY, MI

Somerset Mall, Troy, MI

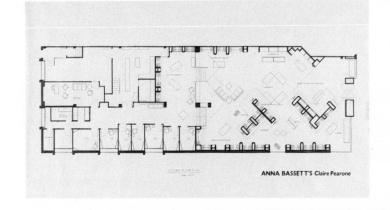

ANNA BASSETT'S Claire Pearone

This redesigned shop was a top award winner in the recent NRMA/ISP store design contest, and starting with its impactful and eloquent marble facade, — one can see why it won the coveted award. The grand architectural entrance statement is faced with imported, colorfully veined Italian marble. The same marble appears inside the store as a fascia band over the wall cases. "The store's interior is defined through geometrically chiseled drops above fashion vignettes and stone-like arches giving focus to the designer coordinates along the walls." The dark gray ceiling echoes the recessed hang-spaces, and the pale gray carpeting washes over the floor, — under simply stated displayer tables and plushy, black leather upholstery.

Above: Stepping down into the rear lower level, — brass rails and glass panels overlook that level and lead the shoppers to Evening Wear. Two vertical shadow display cases are recessed into the black glass wall, and higher priced dresses are featured behind glass doors — and on custom designed fixtures. *Right:* More of the main level and the architectural elements that dominate the design. Display is used to show off an individual piece while the stock is hung in the sectioned-off bays on the wall. The lighting plan combines recessed lamps with focusable spots and MR16 lamps for sparkling high-light accents. The spacious jewelry and accessory cases are beautifully lit from above.

HAROLD Minneapolis, MN

Design:
NORWOOD OLIVER
DESIGN ASSOCIATES
(NODA), NY
Principal:
NORWOOD OLIVER

Project Manager:
MADRAN VAZIRANI
Planning/Merchandising:
DIANE KOESTER
Design:
JOHN BLACKWELL

Color & Materials:
SUSAN STARNES
Photographer:
GEORGE HEINRICH,
MINNEAPOLIS, MN

Shopping in an elegant old mansion would feel just as one feels in this 40,000 sq. ft. retail space that is filled with classic architectural details and decorations, old world moldings, and fine facing materials — used in a grand manner to create a grand style. The shopper enters through glass front doors that reach to "grand" heights to allow the shopper to see what we see on the right. In the main floor foyer, an opulent crystal chandelier hangs down from a vaulted ceiling — enriched with moldings and suffused with soft, hidden light. The walls are also endowed with contrasting moldings or enhanced with damask covered panels. Beyond, see below, one of the exclusive shoe salons.

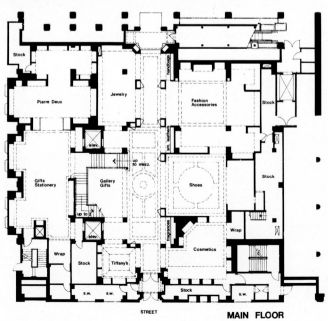

MAIN FLOOR

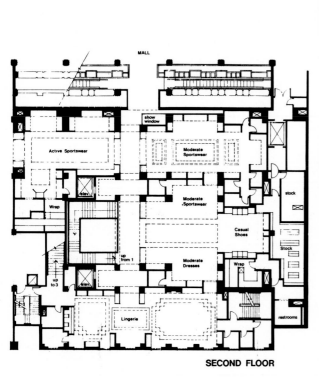

SECOND FLOOR

A staircase connects the first and second levels. "Logic might have taken it up four levels, but esthetics kept it more intimate." Before the store was renovated, customers walked up a rear fire staircase rather than wait for an elevator. In this newly revised design, a back staircase also leads up to all four retail levels but it is now expressed with decorative balustrades, oriental carpeting, crystal chandeliers and tapestries. On the second level, there is a wide open stairwell and surrounding it is a balustrade. Adjacent, under an illuminated, vaulted ceiling is a spacious aisle with entrances into some of the "shops" on this level. The lattice panels (on the left side of the lower left photo) becomes the entrance way into the ready-to-wear shop pictured above. The herring-bone laid wood flooring of the aisle yields to the warm apricot carpeting of the shop.

The "crowning jewel" is found on the fourth level. Conceived like a "Victorian Parlour" is "Couture" with all the amenities a pampered client could wish for. The furnishings are museum pieces and the client is invited to relax in a setting filled with much opulence but little visible merchandise. The merchandise is brought in and "presented." Hallways are framed with creamy marble floors and black columns that make a dramatic presence. Hand carved glass elevator doors (rear) are decorative, and the 10'x10' fitting rooms are generously provided with chandeliers, flattering sconces and every sort of amenity.

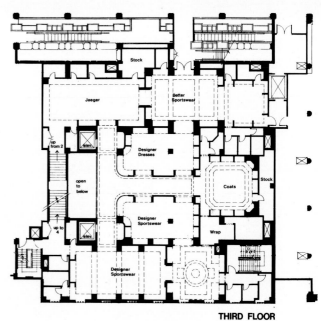

THIRD FLOOR

ALFRED SUNG

Pl. Montreal Trust, Montreal, Quebec, Canada

Store Design:
    KLAUS HAMPEL,
    HAMPEL RETAIL DESIGNS
Visual Merchandising:
    JOAN REDFERN, VISUAL
    PRESENTATION MANAGER
    FOR ALFRED SUNG
Photographer:
    DONIGAN CUMMING

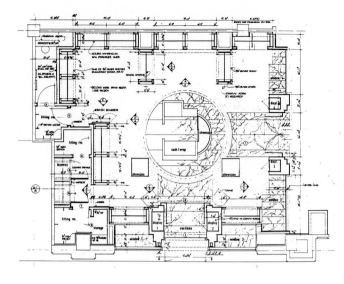

This, the newest of fifteen Sung stores in North America, features the new store concept of Alfred Sung; — a contemporary interpretation of classical architecture and design elements that create a serene and refined setting. The design reflects Sung's "distinctive eye for balance and symmetry, — his affinity for traditions, — and his passion for pure white." The clean lines blend with the harmonious proportions of the areas and the design elements, to create an uncluttered, light and airy feeling. Wide, simple columns are used to delineate distinct areas of the shop and the merchandise is displayed on white custom fixtures, — a combination of bevelled glass, slim fluted columns and a simple entablature. White marble flooring and pale celadon carpeting lead to the marble/glass cash/wrap desk located under a centrally placed, bronze-leafed dome.

23

THALIL

Cours Mont Real, Montreal, Quebec, Canada

Design:
PIERRE PAGE & ASSOC.
MONTREAL

handsome women's specialty store which is fully on view through the wholly glazed storefront. The interior is "boxed off" into convenient, see-through areas by the crossing wood beams overhead and the intersecting wooden paths underfoot. Gray area of carpet indicate the shops. Charcoal metal, floor-to-ceiling posts define the areas and also hold the rod-hung garments. Fine wood fixtures, on the floor and highlighted on the perimeter walls, carry folded and stacked merchandise in this well lit, bright and inviting space.

LA CRICCA-SIMON CHAING

Beaubien, Montreal, Quebec, Canada

Design:
PIERRE PAGE AND
ASSOCIATES, MONTREAL

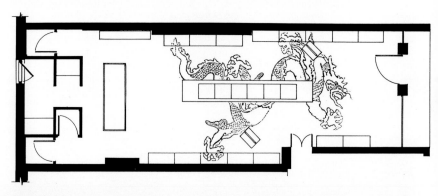

In this, the second of the La Cricca shops, the dragon that is painted on the floor, once again swirls its way around the rectangular plan of the shop. The architectural arch that is the store's facade combines fancifully rendered capitols with sleek, flat surfaces and the walls inside are rendered to simulate coursed ashlar stonework of the 17th cent., Italian renaissance. Natural woods are used for the wall and floor fixtures, and a long painted display table stretches down the center of the store. The lines are contemporary but the inspiration is classic.

LIZ CLAIBORNE
AT JORDAN MARSH Boston, MA

Design:
HAMBRECHT TERRELL
INTERNATIONAL, NY
Principal/Project Director:
JOHN CZORNY

Designer:
GUNJI TACHIKAWA
Lighting Designer:
JANN WEAVER
Senior Planner:
JILL VON SCHLANBUSCH

Decorator:
ADRIENNE ZESSMAN
Photographer:
ROBERT MILLER /
BRADLEY OLMAN

Truly a shop-within-the-store. This 7000 sq. ft. space
was designed as a separate, sleek and contemporary,
upbeat "boutique" in the Woman's area of the store.
Self-contained, it holds Liz Claiborne's four lines:
Collection, Lizsport, Lizwear and Dresses, as well as
the Liz accessories. The mannequins on the four stages
relate to each of the lines and the assorted accessories
are displayed in the rear of the store. A special fixture
was designed by HTI to adapt to the many different
configurations, and display the merchandise in an
exciting, but orderly, manner, — easy for the shopper
to emulate. Very bright lighting and a palette of gray
and white — teamed with natural bleached prima vera
wood and gray stained maple, plus mirrored panels,
make this a "pleasurable, fun place to shop" for the
Liz Claiborne customer.

The mirrored alcoves were designed to give the customer a special space where she can try on her selections and see herself from any angle, — all under the most complementary of lights. The black vertical elements are highlighted with the flattering incandescent lamps that also add a theatrical quality to the space. The same theme is apparent in the Accessories area, in the rear of the shop, that is equipped to complete any of the outfits available up front. The natural prima vera wood is accented with ebony bands, and the woods are used on the roll-about displayer tables as well as the adjustable shelved rear wall. The upper part of the merchandised wall is also mirrored as are the square columns on the floor.

TOPAZ Willowbrook, NJ

Design:
DORF ASSOCIATES, NY
Principal-In-Charge:
MARTIN DORF

Considering the long narrow mall space, the designers, using unique materials, energy saving lighting techniques and flexible store fixtures, were able to create an "energized up-scale image" that was distinctive and fashionable. Perforated metal panels were bent and attached to a steel frame to make the vaulted ceiling that leads up to the elevated shoe salon in the rear. Pre-oxidized copper panels sheathe the columns, on the exterior of the store, capped with burnished stainless steel column capitols. The steel is also used for the sign fascia on the exterior and for facing the vertical piers and dressing room doors facing the terrazzo paved aisle. Here the 18 to 35 year old shoppers find moderate priced clothing in an exhilarating and Continental environment.

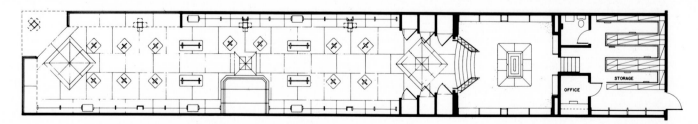

ST. CROIX

900 North Michigan, Chicago, IL

Design
**PHILLIP LE BOY, ARCHITECT,
AIA, SKOKIE, IL**

The store is a prototype designed for a manufacturer of fine women's knitwear, to present the complete line in better retail settings. Most of the small space is on view through the corner glass windows, and the impact of the blue/black, pearlescent granite portico, which is banded with polished chrome, is repeated on the interior pilasters. Halogen wall brackets are used as wash-up lights on the stepped pilasters. Mirrored walls increase the sense of space beneath the stepped coffered ceiling that is illuminated by layers of hidden neon. In addition, there are recessed incandescent lamps used to highlight the perimeter merchandising walls.

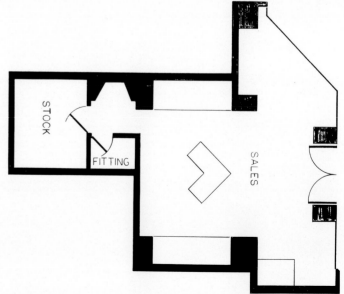

ESPRIT

Sloane St., London, England

Design:
  NORMAN FOSTER &
  ASSOCIATES, LONDON
Structural Engineer:
  ANTONY ROSS, LTD., KENT
Decor/Shopfitters:
  QUICKWOOD, LONDON
Photographer:
  RICHARD BRYANT

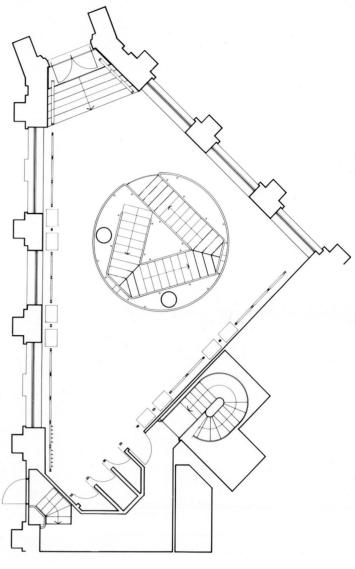

The tight triangular floor space and the use of the basement area created a physical and visual challenge for the architects/designers. In the solution presented here, the lower level is not isolated as a second-grade space, but becomes part of a single vertical space which is centered around a glass staircase. The striking staircase is triangular in plan and reflects the shape of the retail space. The treads are made of 25mm. thick float glass with a sandblasted finish and polished edges. The main construction is fabricated in mild steel box sections, — finished with micaceous iron oxide paint and bolted to 3 no. steel circular section columns. To complete the handsome look, the handrails are made of stainless steel tubing.

Display and storage are set around the perimeter edges of the space and they are sectioned off by vertical, grip-blasted, steel supports, and spced with light birch veneer panels and shelves. For access to the vertically merchandised stock, steel and wood ladders roll along tracks set over the reachable garments. The system allows total flexibility for interior and "large scale window dressing." "The shop is close in spirit to theatre where the actors and the messages are the clothes. In that sense, the neutral range of natural finishes, raw concrete, unpainted metal and timber together with a flexible lighting system provide an appropriate and tuneable stage set."

THE LIMITED Northland Mall, Columbus, OH

Design:
SPACE DESIGN
INTERNATIONAL
CINCINNATI, OH
Principal in Charge:
KEVIN R. ROCHE

Design Director:
LORI WEGMAN
Project Designer:
KATHLEEN A. LISTERMANN
RANDI E. BAYER

For The Limited:
CHARLES HINSON
PRES./STORE PLANNING

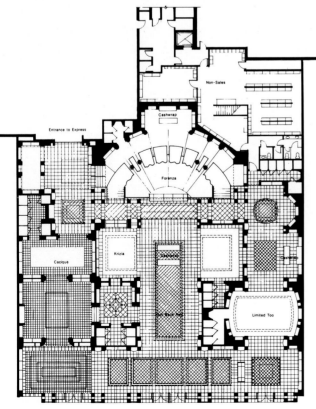

"The design challenge was to create a 'superstore' which would be consistent with The Limited's division's sophisticated, fashionable and savvy personality, and which also communicate the multiple brand personalities that exist within the merchandise strategy." The challenge was met in the 17,000 sq. ft. space with a defined architectural vocabulary that was the backbone of the store's design. The architectural planning considered main and secondary axial paths of circulation combined with specialty shops along the way. To fully develop a "strategic position for communicating the attitude of the multiple merchandise brands," visual display and graphic communication was integrated into the design. *Above:* The central, vaulted main aisle that leads to the apsidial location of Forenza, — with shops along the way.

The spectacular Forenza area is at the far end of the shop — and the axis, and makes a bold, sweeping "Italian" statement. The upper loggia of the two storey space is treated with a rusticated stone pattern interrupted by arched display niches. The lower loggia carries the Italian imported knitwear in contemporary perimeter wall housings. On the patterned marble floor, that follows a radiating pattern under the ceiling skylight, Corinthian capitols are used as displayer tables and platforms.

Below: One of the "specialty shops" in the superstore; Limited Too which carries children's wear. The setting is neutral black and white highlighted with bold graphics and colorful displays.

CASUAL CORNER

Union Square, San Francisco, CA

Design:
    ROBERT P. GERSIN
    ASSOCIATES, INC., NY
Design Team:
    INGRID G. CARUSO
    SARA ARNOLD
    SAMUEL BLAY
    SCOTT BOLESTRIDGE
    ETIENNE MA
    ELIZABETH SANCHEZ
    ROBIN TOLUD
For Casual Corner:
    NOEL DAVIDSON, PRES.
    SPECIALTY   RETAILING
Photographer:
    SHARON RISEDORPH
    SAN FRANCISCO

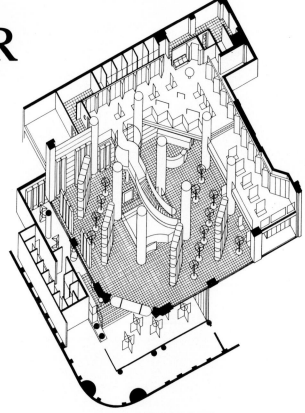

The recently completed major renovation of the Casual Corner flagship store on Union Square has given a new sense of drama and impact to one of the nation's largest Women's Specialty retailers. This store, according to the principal of the design firm — Robert Gersin, "was particularly challenging because we had to maintain the overall Casual Corner image within a 13,000 sq. ft., multi-level space housed in a landmarked building. The program required the use of all our disciplines, — architecture, graphic design, product design, and, of course, interior design." The storefront is "transparent" and sections of glass alternate with areas of limestone to suggest the masonry work of the original building. Both the store's front and the entry are two storeys high.

The soaring space of the multi-level interior is dominated by a sweeping, curved grand staircase, — contemporary in design, that graciously invites the shoppers to sample the fashions found on either the lower level, — or up on the mezzanine. As the shopper is moved through the selling space, she is able to view the surrounding merchandise, and that increases the opportunity for multiple sales.

The materials used are the "signature" elements of the prototype that is appearing in the cross-country renovations of Casual Corner shops; high gloss white enamel and polished copper fixtures and peach and gray marble floors in basically off-white spaces. The ash wall elements give the store a cohesive, feminine and contemporary palette that flatter both the merchandise and the customer. The feature module display, see the previous page, and the moveable wall displays were redesigned from the usual 8½' to 17' tall, and they were combined with three new custom fixture concepts; the triangular rack, the lighted round rack, and a cross fixture which lends a unique quality to the retail setting.

ROBIN KAY 900 North Michigan, Chicago, IL

Design:
   KEIR BROWNSTONE &
   CHICAGO DESIGN GROUP

Concept:
   KENNEY NICKERSON
Construction:
   CHICAGO DESIGN GROUP

Photographer:
   MARTIN M. PEGLER

Robin Kay, the Canadian designer had a mission; provide the marketplace with versatile, simple clothing made of 100% cotton knits. Being both the supplier and the retailer has allowed the Robin Kay organization to avoid restrictive marketing schemes and allowed them to rely more on the designer's fashion instincts. The fashions are color statements, — and since color is what sells, the retail setting is neutral gray and white with black accents. The small space is dramatically and beautifully lit only with MR16, low voltage, tungsten lamps, and that allows the well-stacked and displayed merchandise to step forward in the space — and greet the shopper through the open, glazed facade.

FOLIC

Rua Visc. de Piraja, Rio de Janiero, Brazil

Design:
THE FOLIC ORGANIZATION
Photographer:
Martin M. Pegler

Folic is a fine, fashion-aware shop for the more traditionally-oriented woman. Located in many of the up-scaled malls around Rio, we are featuring the 600 sq. ft. shop on the fashionable shopping street in Impanema. The compact space is finished in a warm white, walls and floors, with contemporary styled, versatile, wood floor fixtures. The simple but attractive wood wall system can accommodate hang rods, shelves, enclosed cabinets and displays. Incandescent, low-voltage lamps are used to supplement the light that filters in through the mainly glass front of the shop.

STUDIO LA RUE

Broadway, NYC

Design:
   Design Clubs, NY
Designer:
   GEOFFREY HASSMAN
Project Manager
   JEAN PAUL CROMBECQUE
Painting & Wall Finishes:
   PETER PETRUCCI
Cabinet Work/Special
Architectural Effects:
   WILLI JUANCA
Color Coordinator:
   BYRON KIETH BYRD

Studio La Rue was conceived as a total women's specialty store made up of different looks, different attitudes — and each was to have its own unique theme. The designer was limited only by the spacious 10,000 sq. ft. of space — on one level — but as for "inspiration" — styles and periods, — he was free to wander back to the ancient Roman Empire, stop off at a Mayan temple — or take off into the next century and visit Krypton. The space is divided with twenty foot tall square, supporting columns that reach from the stained wood floor to the trompe l'oeil painted ceiling above. In between, eighteen, 14' Roman columns create a Roman Empire area, and two changing rooms, like tents of old, add to the decor. Also visible, below, is the centrally located, stepped pyramid.

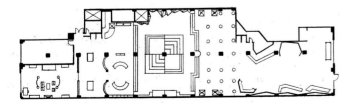

The shopper enters into the Deconstruction Department which houses most of the store's fashion accessories, the bag check, and checkout counter. The racking system is made on actual steel girders placed at angles about the stuccoed walls that are "crumbling" away to reveal the brick-work beneath. Also revealing — is the Segal-esque "plasterer" in white (*far right*) who "moons" the unsuspecting patrons. The jewelry counter flows out of a purple niche and is covered with steel plates.

Far left: The Ice Age not only cometh — it has arrived! The diagonally angled metal tubes of irridescent pink repeat the slashes and faceted angles of the "crystal" walls and dressing rooms. The pink lightening rods lead into the Mosaic area with a green pagoda as its focal point. In addition to the patterned tile floor and curved ledge, there are architectural forms that add to the fireworks of the shop. *Above,* a Gothic fragment in the Mosaic area and another of the trompe l'oeil painted walls behind it.

55

BARNEYS CO/OP W. 17th St., Chelsea, NY

Design:
ROSENBLUM - HARB
ARCHITECTS
Principal-In-Charge:
JAMES HARB, AIA

Project Architect:
CHRISTOPHER POWELL
Building Architects:
BEYER, BLINDER, BELLE, NY

Photographer:
PAUL WARCHOL, NY

The CO/OP caters to women of all ages and presents a mix of "avant garde," moderately priced designer fashions. It is located in a rehabbed tenement building that is part of the expanded Barneys Store for Women in the Chelsea area that is now witnessing a renaissance. Using the multi-level space of 8000 sq. ft., — with a central opening, — the designers have evolved a series of floating retail levels with open vistas that put all the assembled merchandise on view. The neutral color schemed interior is capped with a lattice "ceiling" that obliterates the actual painted-out ceiling above. In addition to activewear and sportswear, the space contains cosmetics, shoes and fashion accessories.

MEN'S SPECIALTY STORES

The Peacock Revolution of the Sixties has come and gone and now as we sit on the threshold of the last decade of this century we are finally seeing the fruits of that Revolution. The stirrings of the '60s called to men to stand up and be selective, — be who and what they wanted to be, — and to dress for the parts they wanted to play. The Revolution offered options, — choices; it opened up the wonderful world of Fashion, and dared to suggest that there was a life after the three button, three piece, gray flannel suit. Men were called to rise up, — to unshackle themselves from the bindings of starched white shirts and dull and dreary ties. To what avail? The result was a rash of flamboyant and outrageous Hawaiian shirts and polyester leisure suits.

But times, — they have changed! Men, — as a group, are no longer a herd, — a mindless, tasteless entity that follows without questioning, — without looking for what is new and different. There has been a proliferation of menswear publications; magazines that have targeted in on specific age groups and lifestyles, — gone beyond Esquire and GQ to find their niches. Newspapers offer men's fashion supplements as frequently as they offer women the opportunity to see the current trends and fashions. Designers of women's couture clothes have stretched over into menswear, and brought even more choices — more options — more selections. The Menswear shop in a department store has become a "world," — a store within-the-store, — an area apart, often composed of shops-within-the shop that offer special looks, unique styling and different approaches to dressing. Retailers are opening stores for specialized retailing concepts like Henry Grethel Studio where one can take a relaxing course in the fine art of casual dressing. This is casual beyond jeans. This dress-up/casual idea is just right for the lifestyle that goes from a baseball game in the sunshine to dinner at dusk and dancing in the dark. For the traditional shopper there are traditional shops rich in wood, brass and marble, and endowed with the grace and refinement of 18th cent. furniture and architectural details, but interpreted with contemporary flair and panache. For the daring, the retailers who dare have found designers who can create exciting environments that are avant garde and trendy — but pleasing. Mannequin platforms and ledges are appearing as integral parts of the store's design, and display helps the man put an outfit together where there is no one available to guide him. Good visual merchandising puts the parts together by style and color. The shopper can't make a mistake, and he can make his own look — in safety.

Time was when men's shops looked like restricted clubs; heavy in velvet and leather, dotted with nailheads, and badly in need of illumination. They were comfortable and they were "the un-changing of the old guard." They represented the status quo in styling, and buying a suit meant getting a replacement or a reasonable facsimile. Today, buying a suit is an experience, — an adventure, — a time for role acting and dressing the part. Color is a vital part of men's fashions and though there are still the neutrals, they too breathe a new life in patterns, prints and fibers.

For some time, the male shopper has been aware of the variety of shopping environments available to women, and now he too has the chance to choose. Emancipation is the freeing of man, — the releasing of man into the marketplace where he can be whoever he chooses to be, — and wear the clothes to prove it. Our selections indicate the many ways to a man's ego, — through creative store design.

Left: Nathaniel & James, Bayside, Miami, FL.

NATHANIEL & JAMES Bayside, Miami, FL

Design:
ECHEVERRIA DESIGN
INTERNATIONAL,
MIAMI, FL

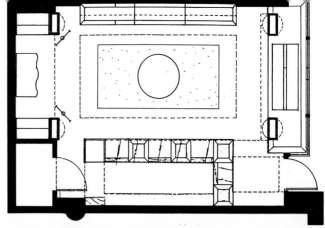

The wide open glass facade gives full access into the wood fixtured, traditional, mens accessory shop that gleams with brass accents. The two angled, furniture units, up front, serve as easels for shirts and ties, and do similar display duty for the inside of the shop. The back wall of the shop is mirrored and an enriched soffit surrounds the raised ceiling that is washed with light. The shirt and tie wall stretches the space and also shows and stocks merchandise effectively. The drawer units, below, contain ties in neat, orderly bins. Throughout, the lighting is warm and low-keyed, but the displays are highlighted for extra emphasis.

BEAU BRUMMEL SPORT Columbus Ave., NYC

Design:
  SPITZER & ASSOCIATES, NY
Associate in Charge:
  FREDERICK S. CLAPPER

Project Team:
  HAROLD SPITZER
  FREDERICK CLAPPER
  ANDY SHAPRIO

Photographer:
  GEORGIANA BEDROSIAN, NY

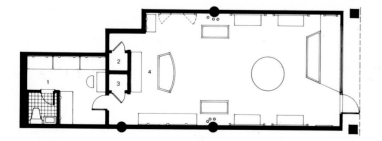

In keeping with the Beau Brummel concept, oak panels were used, but black trim, — carpeting and trapezoidal shaping — both in wall and free standing fixtures, created a different look for this 700 sq. ft. shop which showcases sportier goods and lower priced sportswear than the traditional B.B. store. Track lighting is supplemented by custom chandeliers and sconces to provide bright and sharp lighting. The walls and floor are a soft, gray to complement the colorful merchandise and the oak wood.

BEAU BRUMMEL Madison Ave., NYC

Design:
SPITZER & ASSOCIATES,
ARCHITECTS, NY
Associate in Charge:
FREDERICK S. CLAPPER

Project Team:
HAROLD SPITZER
FREDERICK CLAPPER
TIMOTHY NISSEN

Photographer:
GEORGIANA BEDROSIAN, NY

Elegance is the keynote of this 1775 sq. ft. space, on two levels. The designers took signature elements of former Beau Brummel shops, — oak panelling, cabinets and floors, — light walls and semi-traditional trims and details, — and further refined them for this Madison Ave. location. An etched glass screen partitions off the mezzanine, and it is enhanced by the custom brass railing. Up here, private showings are arranged. The expanded tie display, up front, adds textural interest to the design as well as sells the merchandise.

OLIVER

Rome, Italy

Design:
  DDA, DAVID DAVIES
  ASSOCIATES, LONDON

Oliver is a new fashion label created by the couture house of Valentino to appeal to the younger, style-conscious individual. The collection is based on classic clothing — with a twist — to create an original and individual look. The 18th century building that was formerly an art gallery, was converted into three fashion rooms which blend classic with contemporary design. The entrance sets the tone; a modern bronze shopfront set into the original carved travertine marble portico. Inside, fine blonde maple panels are accented with satin chrome studs, halogen lights are cantilevered off the wall systems, and floors are paved in granite or laid with wood or capreted. Arches and other architectural details of the original structure are used to enhance the new/old, classic/contemporary dichotomy of the design.

MALLARD SPORT N. Michigan Ave., Chicago, IL

Design:
   JON ROBERTS
   ASSOCIATES, INC.
   SAN FRANCISCO, CA
Project Design:
   MANUEL ENCARNACION
Visual Merchandiser:
   JACK
   KREITINGER
Photographer:
   JIM NORTH

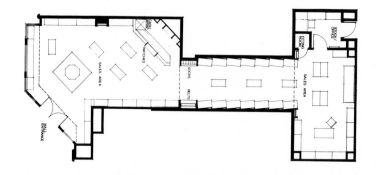

Located in the new Avenue Atrium that is dominated by the Bloomingdales (also reviewed in this edition), is this handsome Men's Specialty store. The designers had to contend with a rather odd T-shaped floor plan. The 1300 sq. ft. space is divided into a rectangular area with the actual entrance cater-cornered on that rectangle, and two long, narrow spaces forming the "T." The shop front is a "greenhouse" of natural wood and glass with angled glass panels above to allow in light from the atrium. Display vignettes fill the window areas and inside, on a round table, the shopper is greeted by another display presentation.

Above: The wood display floor fixtures are diagonally set on the diagonally laid white oak floor, — behind the round table previously shown. Behind them — following the same diagonal, is the cash/wrap desk that directs the shopper to the long narrow, merchandised aisle that ends with the slash of the "T." A fascia of green makes a decorative accent in an otherwise off-white and natural wood environment. The molding is Shaker-inspired and the wood dowel trim is spaced twelve inches apart. On the rear wall, seen in close-up on the left, is a special fixture that adds to the architectural quality of the store design, and also provides an important focal point at the end of the store. The visual merchandising and display is enhanced by the generous arrangement of focusable, incandescent spots in addition to the recessed lamps. Green glass drop lights, over the cash/wrap desk, restate the green accent color and also lights up the counter top. The wood display shelving is by Lundia.

HENRY GRETHEL STUDIO

Water Tower Pl., Chicago, IL

Design:
THE DE PALMA GROUP,
CHICAGO
V.P. in Charge:
ELSA S. DE PALMA

Designer:
BERNADINO MERCADE
Lighting Consultant:
LIGHTING BY DESIGN,
NORTHBROOK, IL

Photographer:
A.Y. SATO
SATO PHOTOG.

The design concept for the store evolved from the merchandise, and the merchandise is men's urban weekend sportswear, — dress-up, casual clothes. It was decided to present the collection in a "life-style concept," and still maintain the identity of the designer of the line of garments. Color stories and wardrobe dressing appeal had to be easily apparent. Thus, the space was designed to simulate the ambience of an artist's studio loft; to identify with the Henry Grethel Studio label. The store is subtley divided into "rooms," — individualized areas furnished with floor fixtures that complement the classic Prairie and Mission styles of furniture. The eclectic mix of floor fixtures works to affect the casual feeling desired for the sportswear, and also helps to arrange the merchandise with a "wardrobe-logic." The furniture and accessories enhance the residential aspect of the design concept. Real artwork also enhances the special personality of the client and the shop.

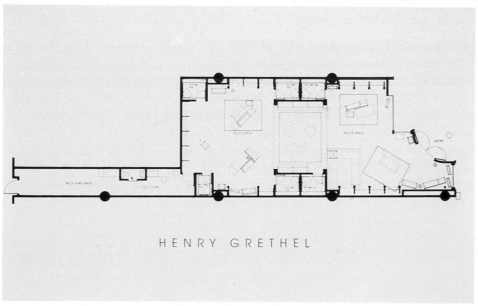

HENRY GRETHEL

The rich woods, both on the floors and the wall furniture, establish the sense of a "man's place." Display vignettes are not out on area rugs and the floor fixtures resemble furniture. *Right:* One of the selling areas with two chairs and a table, and a bookcase wall beyond stacked and hung with color coordinated garments. Increasing the "loft" look are the wooden trusses that span the space and the white canvas baffles that hand down from the high ceiling. The lighting mixes the architectural styling of a lighted vault with state-of-the-art quartz track fixtures. The fitting rooms are spacious, and also well lit. The Home-look calls for and receives an ample provision of green plants in simple terra-cotta pots.

KODO

Kings Road, London, England

Store Design:
PORTLAND DESIGN
ASSOCIATES, LONDON
Principal-in-Charge:
DAVID D'ALMADA

Designer:
NICOLA MALLETT
Store Fixturing:
RAPIER SYSTEM
Store Fitting Contractor:
CIL SHOPFITTERS, LONDON

The designers were challenged to create a Japanese feeling for the 1500 sq. ft. store that sells Japanese label merchandise. The interior has free standing box panels around the main walls, decorated in white, into which is inserted a merchandising system with a raw steel finish. In contrast to the parchment colored walls, there is slate on the window display area and gray Amtico tiles for the rest of the store's flooring. The white tiled ceiling is accented by a stepped down area, in gray, on one side of the shop. The cash/wrap counter, the display tables and the shopfront fascia are all trimmed with a light Japanese elm finish.

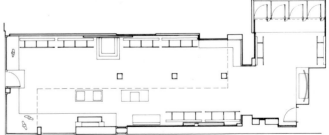

J. RIGGINGS

Tri-County Mall, Cincinnati, OH

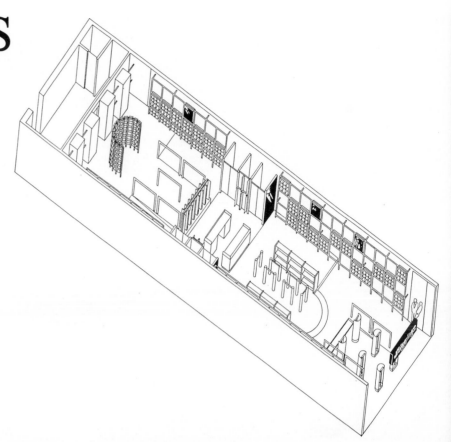

Design:
  ROBERT P. GERSIN
  ASSOCIATES, NY
Custom Fixtures:
  CONCEPT   PLASTICS,
  CINCINNATI, OH &
  ONTARIO STORE FIXTURES,
  WESTON, ONTARIO, CANADA
Environmental Graphics:
  AMBASSA DOR ARTS, NY
  HADLEY EXHIBITS,
  BUFFALO, NY
Photographer:
  MICHAEL DATOLI

This prototype design was initiated to "reposition" the J. Rigging chain of Men's specialty stores. The original store design had become outdated and had failed to keep pace — and face — with the shoppers and their changing fashion attitudes and awareness. The design we are featuring was created "to attract the traditionally reluctant shopper." The first and most evident change came with the redesign of the store's facade; now a completely open and inviting storefront which incorporates the new signage and graphics that are an integral part of the "repositioning." The entrance also features a "first-of-kind," back-illuminated, Duratron images of two figures in casual apparel — on one side, and tailored on the other. The duality in Menswear today, tailored and casual, plays an important part in the store design concept, and it is repeated in the environmental graphics within, as well as on the shopping bags and boxes that leave the store. For the color scheme of the store, the designers selected black lacquered and dark green enamelled metals combined with maple for the fixturing; the walls, where visible, are off white. The carpet is pin-dotted, gray nylon.

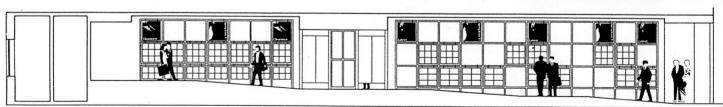

To further enhance the contemporary masculine look in the shop, the ceiling is panelled in warm pine wood with a poly-urethane finish. The ceiling is patterned with fluorescent luminaires and recessed incandescent lamps. As indicated in the sectional views below, — and explained in the photo on the left, the shop is purposefully built on an incline — in a series of rising plateaus that gradually and easily draw the shoppers to the rear of the store where the more tailored clothes and accessories are stocked with style. The custom designed, semi-circular shirt fixtures make an apsidial end to the shop, and it is visible from the front of the store because of its elevated position. Also from the front, thanks to the 3' incline, the shopper can see the whole store and the plan that adapts from one or two major merchandise statements to as many as ten smaller ones. A grid system, permanently installed on the side walls, supports side hanging and stocking as well as the important graphic panels.

EXTENSION

The Galleria, White Plains, NY

Design:
  VINICK ASSOCIATES
  HARTFORD, CT
Designer:
  BERNARD S. VINICK,
  FASID, CHAIRMAN
Photographer:
  WARREN JAGGER

The challenge to be met in the layout of this very narrow, very deep space of just over 2000 sq. ft., was to make a presence felt that this was something new, young and exciting — and to make that impact in a large, urban mall. This is the first "extension" for an existing small chain of men's stores operating under the new name. In presenting the line of essentially Euro-

pean manufactured men's clothing and accessories, ensembles had to be creatively displayed as guides for the shoppers, and a great variety of merchandise had to be housed efficiently. Using black and gray with subtle variations, the designers did create a clean masculine look, and the accent color was used in the logo-signage outside and inside the store.

AVVENTURA

Water Tower Pl., Chicago, IL

Design:
    GREEN, HILTSCHER,
    SHAPIRO, LTD., CHICAGO, IL
Photographer:
    JAMIE PADGETT,
    KARANT & ASSOC. INC.

The relatively small space of about 800 sq. ft., plus the existing 30'' round column directly at the center of the store front, and a modest budget presented unique design challenges to the designers. The structural column, at the center, was turned into a striking design element, — and incorporated into bulbous gridded facade. The same motif is repeated on the rear wall of the shop with great success. "These columns provide a focal for the eye, and physically become the framework for display and sales." The products are highly visible and physically within reach of the customer. The store features over 200 styles of boots and shoes and has storage space for 1500 more pair — all in the subdued and elegant deep gray interior.

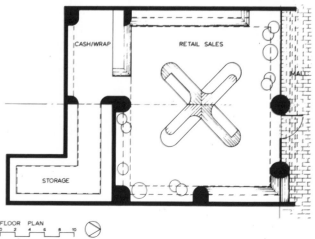

FLOOR PLAN
0 2 4 6 8 10

LIFE-STYLE

This chapter could be subtitled "Specialty stores as Department Stores" — just as our Department Store chapter could be subtitled "Department Stores as Specialty Stores." This chapter is about specialty stores that sell to both men and women — in the same retail space.

Life-Style — a way of living — of thinking — of doing things. It is a way of making fashion decisions. It has only been in the last few years that the equality of the sexes has arrived with a whole string of acronyms like Yuppies, Bubbies and Dinks. It is boys and girls together; living and enjoying together, — shopping together, sharing mutual tastes, attitudes — and designer labels. It is not a completely new phenomenon, but it is a stimulating concept and a form of retailing that is becoming more and more popular. It is Life-Style that has made shopping a "shared experience." The "boys and girls together" theory in retailing permits them to get the same pleasure out of this shared time in the market. It's not where he has to dawdle — hop from one foot to the other — while she seems to be spending a lifetime rummaging through endless miles of racks, — or she politely sits and stares at her perfect cuticles or the ceiling while he tries on jacket after jacket. Now they can be shopping, looking, selecting and rejecting at the same time — in the same place — for merchandise that speaks of a particular way of life — or for a designer that appeals to a certain group of shoppers. What makes this concept of selling menswear and womenswear of the same fashion attitude or style in the same shop so satisfying is the interaction that is possible between "he" and "she" — in adjacent shops — in eye contact with each other.

This sort of shopping has been going on for some time in Europe — and some of the more trendy shops in Japan, in Tokyo, have also been dividing up their shops by designer, — by life-style, — by fashion attitude rather than by sex. Just as teens "date" in the malls and shop the shops, so do the more mature couples, and the more affluent ones, take pleasure in shopping excursions together. If they are Polo-oriented, in their tastes, they will prefer finding Polo Women next to Polo Men, rather than finding them levels apart with Polo Women as a boutique in the Women's area on two, and Polo Men as a separate shop in the Men's department, — down on the main level.

Our selections come from Europe, from Canada, Latin America and from assorted cities across the United States. We have top designer shops like Gianni Versace, Issey Miyake, Yamamoto and Valentino where couples can and do shop together. For other kinds of life-style dressing there is Bogner, Express and Phillipe Martin. Sophisticated and very up-scale shoppers will find their mutual needs and tastes satisfied in Tootsies, Quinto and Le Player. For the daring, the trendy, for those who find dressing fun and games — where they can mix and match, — there is Mexx and Le Chateau.

It's a good idea getting the sexes together in one space — and keeping them there — interested and involved. Eventually they make their decisions and purchases — together.

Left: Tootsies, Highland Village, Houston, TX.

TOOTSIES

Highland Village S/C, Houston, TX

Interior Design:
ALSEY W. NEWTON, JR., AIA
Project Architect:
CHARLES A. HUBBARD, AIA

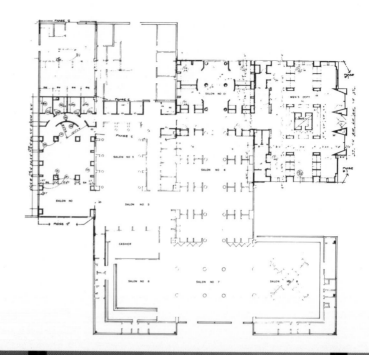

Tootsies' owner, Mickey Rosmarin, teamed up with his designers to create a shop which would provide a memorable and distinctive background for the designer clothes to be carried. The result is a handsome, elegant structure filled with classic materials, used with classic restraint. The desired look was to suggest the feeling of a 1910 Parisian museum; a combination of European Art-Deco and Viennese Bauhaus. The black marble tiled floors and the ebony colored cases and counters add a sleek, sophisticated quality to the space that is dominated by a double colonnade made of off-white columns. The shopper is lead through the aisle under a softly illuminated, vaulted ceiling. Tall folding screens serve as partitions between areas on the floor, and also serve as backgrounds for mannequins dressed in fashions by Ungaro, Montana, Thierry Mugler, LaCroix, and other notables.

Above: The Men's accessory area, on the black marble floor under the "Viennese skylight." The store now encompasses 25,000 sq. ft. of retail space, and includes an expanded women's couture, women's contemporary clothes, shoes, cosmetics and lingerie boutiques, as well as the Men's shop.

QUINTO

St. Catherine St., Montreal, Quebec, Canada

Design:
 THE INTERNATIONAL DESIGN
 GROUP, TORONTO
Executive Vice President:
 R. MAC LACHLIN
Architect & Designer:
 NELLA FIORINO

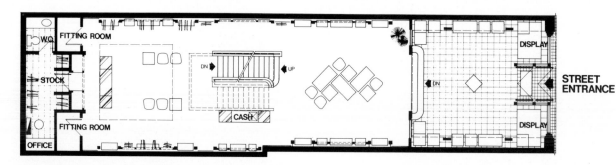

GROUND FLOOR PLAN

This space, — 5300 sq. ft. — on three levels — incorporates three distinct functions. First and foremost, it is a retail environment that specializes in high fashion Women's and Men's shoes and accessories, as well as some ready-to-wear. The space also houses a showroom and the corporate office headquarters — all under one roof with one identity. For the design reference, — the physical image that would relate to the shopper who and what Quinto is, — the designers opted for a late 20th century interpretation of the classical elements of design, details and elegance that added a sense of grandeur to 19th cent. residences. The two storey high storefront is a black framed, luminous glass wall that is anchored to the facade — and serves also to separate this store from its surroundings. It was designed not only to feature the courtyard entrance, but also to allow for maximum visual and light penetration from the street; to allow the shopper to sample the building's interior styling from without. As shown on the floor plan, above, the shopper enters into a tiled courtyard that rises two storeys high — wanders past displays on ledges — then proceeds up a few stairs into the Women's Accessory area with its commodious seating arrangements.

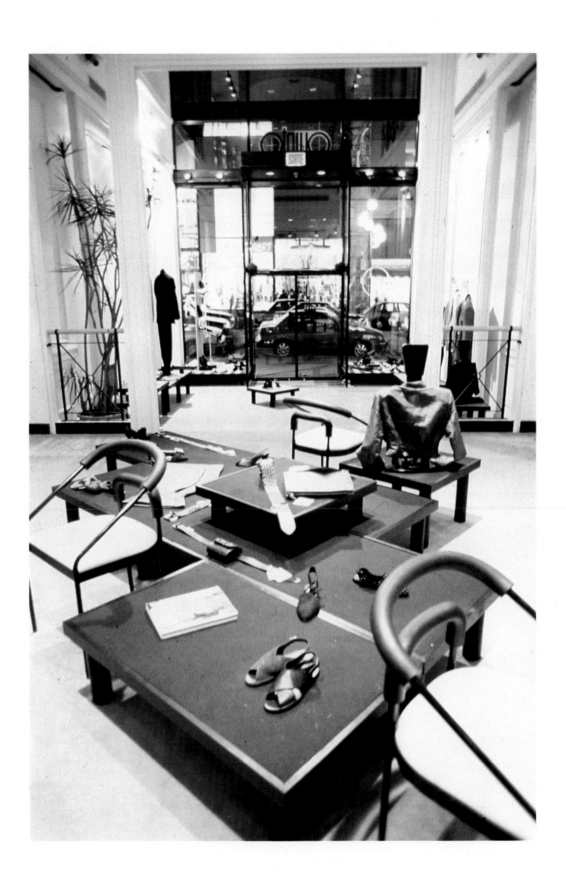

Left: A view from the 20' x 20' courtyard looking into the elevated main level of the store. Behind, center, is the staircase that links the three floors into a continuous entity.

The simple contrasting color scheme consists of ivory, natural fleshtone finished wood, stone and carpeting — complemented with black accents that act as a frame or background for the merchandise and also emphasizes the sense of scale. The black elements point up the serenity — and drama — that enfolds within the various retail areas. The mezzanine, above, is centrally located within the building and has a balustraded balcony at one end with a view of the courtyard — and open to the light that comes through the window areas. Because of code restrictions, only 40% of the existing second floor space could be used and thus the open area is a decorative plus in the design scheme. The black flattened arches and vertical elements provide the detailing to the otherwise unadorned walls and the wood frames outline and contain the merchandise presentations. The low slung arch motif also appears in the facade design.

SECOND FLOOR PLAN

In the Men's area on the second level, and again the look into the courtyard and the entrance into the store. The placement of the grand stairway towards the back of the building not only acts as a central axis to unite the three levels, it also serves as a focal point that brings the shopper towards the rear of the long, narrow space. The staircase is elegantly detailed with black enamelled ornamental ironwork and oak flesh-tone railings. In addition, aligned with the staircase is a large rooftop skylight that allows in the natural light to be diffused and refracted throughout all three levels. This brings new dimension and life to the "darkest" corners of the shop. In the photo, left, one can again appreciate the use of the flattened arch motif combined with classically inspired piers and moldings. The same design elements are visible on either side wall of the courtyard beyond.

The designers attempted and succeeded in "creating an interior of sophisticated simplicity."

GIANNI VERSACE

Crocker Galleria, San Francisco, CA

Design:
**LABORATORIO
ASSOCIATI OF MILAN**

On the two levels of Crocker Galleria, the shopper can find the Versace boutiques for Men and Women — and the complete collections of the innovative fashion designer. From the open glass facade and throughout the retail space, there is a sense of spaciousness, and the rich facing materials are used with taste and discretion. Nothing is blatant or obvious here. The client enters into the women's area (right) and is immediately transported to an Italian, high-fashion environment with walls that echo classic architectural elements and motifs in a simple, contemporized manner. The Men's area, below, is enriched with keystoned arches that open into spacious dressing rooms. The textured wall, opposite the arches, is divided into bays that combine restrained face-out hanging with shelves of folded garments.

YOHJI YAMAMOTO USA, INC.

Grand St., NYC

Design:
   ALAIN MUNKITTRICK OF
   MUNKITTRICK ASSOC.,
   NEWTON, MA

Metal Fixture/Screens:
   ANTONY DONALDSON,
   LONDON

Metal Sculptures:
   JOHN CRISFIELD
   TIMOTHY HINE
   JAMES HORROBIN

Photographer:
   KATARINA BLAZEVIC

This 3000 sq. ft. store in NYC's Soho district holds the Yamamoto collection of men's and women's fashions. It is the first store in the United States for Yamamoto, and the design concept was inspired by architectural supplies and graphic arts materials. Sculptures serve not only as decorations, they also function as fixtures, dividers and architectural detailings. The unusual forged iron racks contrast with the fluid lines of the clothes and the hand wrought iron screen separates the men's area from the women's — technically but not visually. According to the designers, the "warmth" of this loft space comes from the use of steel, bronze and exotic hardwoods like Brazilian walnut and ebony. Natural light floods the white-walled space as it streams in through the eleven monumental windows that wrap around the selling area.

ISSEY MIYAKE

Madison Avenue, NYC

Store Design Concept:
  TOMIO MOHRI
Interior Design:
  SHIRO KURAMATA
Architecture:
  TOSHIKO MORI, AIA
Lighting:
  MASAO NIHEI
Photographer:
  MIKIO SEKITA

Miyako, the designer, is unique. His clothes are "declarations of independence for the body and challenge so many traditions, — break so many rules, — that they need different standards to be understood or even worn." For his exclusive showroom for men's and women's wear he needed an architectural statement that would provide the right setting for his highly individual fashions — and set them off. This shop is an excellent example of the creative best in contemporary Japanese store environments.

A staircase of industrial textures and materials creates a chasm in the diagonally boxed, terrazzo floor, and following the line of the stairway is an inverted V that extends down from the ceiling. The long line of the space is stretched even more by the track lighting that provides the ambient and focal lighting for the floor. A corrugated textured wall is the background for the gar-

ments hung on steel cables that swoop through the
space, and that same texture fronts the cash/wrap
counter.

The only pale touch of color is on the triple screen,
on the rear wall, behind the unusual table made of
textured gray wood and white laminate, with the
merchandise on display under a tunnel of lucite. The
spare, uncluttered shop makes an impactful impression.

103

VALENTINO

Paris, France

Design:
**DDA, DAVID DAVIES
ASSOCIATES, LONDON,
ENGLAND**

On the Ave. Montaigne, this is the recently redesigned Valentino Boutique for men and women. Using natural woods, marble and chrome details, the designers have brought in a new look to serve as a background for the elegant collections. Sparkling curved glass rod screens in the window, — open into a double height marble hall which is lined with marble dust walls accented with a frieze of chrome disks. From here, six full height pivoting mirrors mark the transition into the softer, more luxurious environment of the ladies couture area.

Inside the couture rooms, the collections line the walls with the items displayed behind pivoting glass screens. A curving accessory wall leads to a column lined gallery which is also enhanced by tall mirrors and a long sweep of carpet. The curved wall features the cash desk which serves as a directional force connecting the men's and women's areas. Throughout there is the exquisite care to detailing and the interplay between high-tech and high-class materials and design elements.

LE PLAYER

The Waterways, N. Miami Beach, FL

Design:
ECHEVERRIA DESIGNS
INTERNATIONAL,
CORAL GABLES, FL
Principal-In-Charge:
MARIO ECHEVERRIA

In an "up" area, Le Player, in 6000 sq. ft. of space, is a mini-department store for affluent men and women. It is classic and high-tech at the same time as the design combines granite and handsome wall materials with vivid displays of neon art and signage. Fine fixtures blend with relaxed sitting areas and the focal point of the store is a lounge area where men and women can meet, have a drink, watch t.v. and relax before returning to their shopping. "Ensemble assembly" is facilitated by fixtures that hold the fashion accessories next to the garments. There is an elegant flow of design throughout the space which incorporates the neon designs and textured metals within laminated surfaces.

BOGNER

Munich, Germany

Design:
    MARK MACK, PRINCIPAL-
    IN CHARGE
Project Architecture:
    WOOI-CHENG CHOONG
Project Team:
    ERIC CARLSON
    LEIGH SATA
    CHRISTINE MA
    SHAUN WESTON
Associate Architect:
    HEINO STAMM
    PLANUNGBURO,
    BRUCKNER & PARTNERS

The home site of the Munich based manufacturer of upscaled sportswear and ski apparel is Bogner Haus, located in the center of Munich. The four storey shop was remodeled, inside and out, to accommodate to a new, more youthful approach to the company, — and its clients. The first floor is devoted to three functions; the display of fashion in the show windows (*below*), — the stimulation of customers with video displays, — and the cashier's desk. On the other floors, individual corrections were made to the existing structure and a simple but versatile hanging system was designed for merchandise presentation.

The development of this system went with the design of
the store, and shows the use of similar materials in an
eye-catching, rainbow-colored, array of stained ash.
The system is basically a freestanding, wood clad,
column with slotted steel standards as centers. They are
connected to the back wall through a sandblasted bow
which is also an allusion to the company's logo.

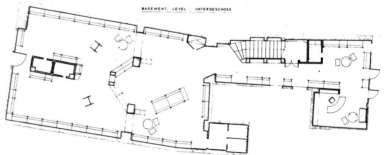

BASEMENT LEVEL · UNTERGESCHOSS

The reorganized interior was centered on the circulation
around the staircase. The staircase is enhanced by the
addition of a wainscoting in red stained ash which
continues as parquet flooring into the upper storeys.
Screening the staircase, the architectural arcade
introduces an element of street architecture into the
interior. *Above:* A view of the men's area, and the wall
system designed for Bogner. The metal "bow" motif
atop the wall fixtures adds a decorative note to the
otherwise straight-lined architectural elements. "The
agile arrangement of elements befits the sporty lifestyle
that the purchase of Bogner attire seemingly carries
with it." (Architectural Record, May '88).

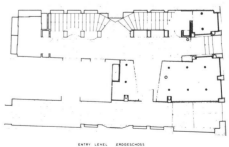

ENTRY LEVEL   ERDGESCHOSS

MEXX
Peter Cornelius Hoofstraat, Amsterdam, Netherlands

Design:
   ROBERT A.M. STERN,
   ARCHITECT
Associate Architect:
   DIK SMEDING, AMSTERDAM
Project Architect:
   ALEX LAMIS
   GRAHAM S. WYATT
Merchandising Designer:
   DAVID DAVIES, ASSOC.,
   LONDON
Lighting Designer:
   CLINE, BETTRIDGE,
   BERSTEIN LIGHT DESIGN, NY
Photographer:
   PETER AARON

The 3000 sq. ft. store on Amsterdam's most fashionable shopping street boasts a storefront with a proscenium arch that suggests, — then leads into the "theatrical experience" within. The layered composition inside, — from front to back, is reminiscent of stage settings, and the lighting carries out that illusion with a chiaroscuro quality that accents individual items rather than washing the entire floor with uniform light. "The architectural forms are both young and aggressive, — in keeping with the company's image."

PHILIPPE MARTIN

Centro, Rio de Janiero, Brazil

Design:
GUILHERME OF
FEITONOS TROPICOS
Photographer:
MARTIN M. PEGLER

One of a chain of up-scaled men's and women's wear shops, this store is located on a busy street in downtown Rio. The store is light, bright and high-tech with many industrial surfacing materials and textures used with great sophistication. The shiny white HVAC system that encompasses the store, overhead, is used to make a design statement as it contrasts with the weathered and corroded textures and colors of the ceiling and the walls. The floor is laid in a crisp gray and white checkerboard, and the centrally located cash/wrap counter is sinuously curved and sheathed in satin steel topped with a charcoal laminate. All the fixtures are custom designed to go with the contemporary, structural concept of the store's design.

114

LE CHATEAU

Fairview Mall, Toronto, Ontario, Canada

Store Design:
    YABU/PUSHELBERG,
    TORONTO, ONT.
Store Set-Up Supervisor:
    M. MAJOR
Display Supervisor:
    D. PARE
Photographer:
    DAVID WHITTAKER

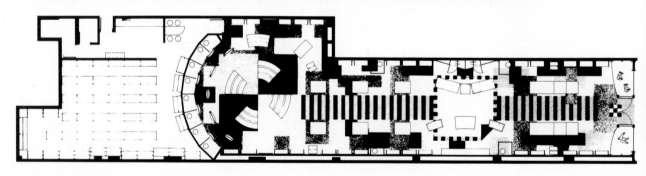

The storefront shows silk-screened images, mounted and raised out on pins and rivets. Graphically signed window displays reinforce the client's request for a strong distinction between the sexes in fashion presentation. The overall view of the store, above, emphasizes the main "raceway." The raceway concept is reinforced by a striped terrazzo and carpet runner, and suspended convex mirrors and track lights on extension wands. Men's and women's merchandise have color coded walls and ceilings. The stepped, lay-down tables create an openness which encourages the shoppers to move on into the store.

Below: A view of the shoe department and the fitting rooms which are located at the end of the "raceway." The four semi-circular tables display shoes and also provide seating for the shoppers. Track fixtures in mono-points, mounted in a circular pattern reinforce the placement of the tables.

Right: The men's area with the wall merchandising system and the stepped display tables off the raceway. Shelves and hang bars are suspended from heavy duty, wall standards and the top panels are filled with oak veneers, with grommets on top from which are suspended the graphic panels and signage. The free standing mirrors are placed against the wall but can be moved forward when the 4' of wall space it occupies is needed for merchandise. The curtain enclosed dressing room also takes up one of the four foot modules of wall space.

COMPAGNIE INTERNATIONALE EXPRESS

Rodeo Dr., Beverly Hills, CA

Design:
  SPACE DESIGN
  INTERNATIONAL
  CINCINNATI, OH

Architect/Designer:
  KEVIN A. ROCHE
  PRINCIPAL-IN-CHARGE
  LORI A. WEGMAN
  ACCOUNT EXECUTIVE
Project Director:
  RANDI E. BAYER

Project Architect:
  DAVID N. FISCHER, AIA
For the Limited:
  CHARLES HINSON
  PRES./STORE PLANNING

The design challenge was to embody and develop the core personality, — and proprietary language — of Express as a French-based, International retailer. Working closely with The Limited's corporate store planner group, the store's design concept was evolved; an authentic French feeling based on French architecture, artists, fashions and culture. The super-scale visuals of French elements add a sense of humor to the store and an "appeal to the younger persons interested in high fashions, international music and 'hip' art."

120

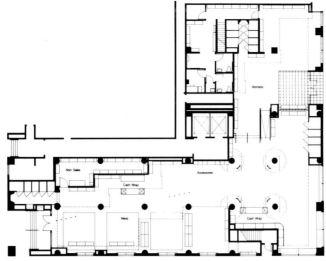

Left: The newly added Men's section. In keeping with the look of the store as an entity, exotic materials were used including black-dyed poplar, purple-heart, and makore woods. Handplastered walls are treated in neutral colors and blue is added as an accent color. In the midst of a very contemporary setting is a Rococo, gold-leafed mirror; a sparkling accent and "reminder" of the French tradition, as is the Napoleon bust on the black lacquered table.

Below: A very Baroque frieze, with the gold orb "engraved" with EXP, over the wood merchandise shelves and stacked bins. In the foreground, a sweater draped sphinx, — another French Empire motif that reappears in other parts of the selling floor. This 7200 sq. ft. space has recently received an award from Monitor, the Shopping Center Industry magazine, in the category of remodeled stores.

FASHION ACCESSORIES

It is the little things that mean a lot, — especially in creating the total fashion look, and it is the small, ultra-specialized fashion accessory shop that often adds so much sparkle and sheen to a mall or shopping street. Often the fashion accessory shop is small in size and filled with choices and selections. It is the store designer's problem to solve; how to create a warm, friendly and inviting ambience with displays and samples that suggest the dept of stock and yet not overwhelm the shopper with so much that she can't find the item because of all the other surrounding items.

We are in a Renaissance of Retailing that has also been called the Boutiquing of America. Affluent and upscale shoppers are searching for stores that offer service, convenient location and hours, and, — an in-depth selection of product. They want ambience, excitement and romance, and always choice. With the cost of good retail space soaring, smaller shops, focused on specialized products seem to be the answer.

Our selections include several examples of this new breed of specialized shop which make their appeal through color, textures, lighting and display. Some are free-standing on revitalized urban streets, — rehabbed to new glory. Others are in malls, in town or out of town. All are selling Fashion Accessories, — the necessary and adaptable handmaidens of Fashion; shoes, bags, belts, scarves and cosmetics. There are several costume jewelry shops which are beginning to appear in generally upscaled malls across the U.S. Impostors is truly classic in appearance, in architectural detailing, color and textures, while Chic exudes a smart sophistication and interplays rich marble surfaces with contemporary lines and angles. For a completely razzle-dazzle effect, D'Mar, down Mexico way, certainly relies on an exciting design statement.

For shoe stores we have truly covered the price and style range: from exclusive and expensive Joan & David and Martinez Valero, to popular priced purveyors of fashions in malls like Hahn Shoes and Tip-Top Shoes, as well as London based Cable & Co. Also in that panorama of choices is a stunning and surprising Goldi in the equally stunning Avenue Atrium in Chicago, and a most unique looking Lucchese Boot Company in San Antonio. Gwen Mazer is the queen of high-style accessories of downtown San Francisco, — but it is a title she shares with the exquisite Hermes shop just across from Union Square. Hermes not only carries the noted shoes and bags and belts, but also luggage, riding equipment, gift items and their world famous scarves. In the small, oddly shaped space, full of angles, is Top 'N' Knot, a smart shop that specializes in hats, ties and scarves. For the finishing touch, — a scent! Floris is a new/old scent shop that just opened a new outlet on Madison Ave. bringing its 250 year old name and English tradition to that fashion street.

The dictionary defines it as follows: "ACCESSORY": (ak-ses-o-ree), noun: a thing that is extra, useful or decorative. Actually, in a fashion sense it is all three — and it is a must. These shops show how a "must" is merchandised with style, and sensitivity for the shoppers.

Left: Chic, Riverside Square Mall, Hackensack, NJ.
Design: David Lloyd Maron, P.C.

GWEN MAZER COLLECTION

Maiden Lane, San Francisco, CA

Architecture/Design:
DAVID COLLEEN /
PETER PETRUZZI

General Contractor:
BENNETT HALL /
MUREALISM
Casework:
POINT DESIGNS

Store Display:
GABRIELLE HENRI
Photographer:
BENNETT HALL

"The Gwen Mazer Collection provides an elegant selection of fashion accessories and assists its clients to develop their own personal style through consulting services, seminars and events." There is a complete collection of semi-precious jewelry, belts, hats, handbags, gloves, shawls and scarves, — all selected by Gwen Mazer, a former fashion editor at Harper's Bazaar. The collection is housed in an elegantly designed and appointed duplex shop of 1200 sq. ft. The main level is connected to the upper service level by a handsome staircase (West Edge Designers, Tony Dominski — designer), and products are displayed in custom designed fixtures under low-keyed, flattering lights.

IMPOSTORS

Embarcadero Center, San Francisco, CA

Design::
    THE METRIX ORGANIZATION,
    ARCHITECTURAL INTERIORS
    COLLA BORATIVE,
    SAN RAMON, CA

"The emphasis at Impostors is in creating the total shopping experience so when you leave the store you have experienced buying a very expensive item when, in fact, you spent only fifty to seventy-five dollars," says Nancy Olsen, president of the chain of twenty-two, elegantly classic shops on the West Coast. Asymmetrically arranged classical architectural elements create a classy/contemporary entrance into the store. Inside, the classical elements and architectural elements dominate in the warm, glowing setting. The rose/peach color appears on the walls, the carpet and the coffered ceiling. A "broken" fluted column, centrally located, is an arresting muesum case — spotlighted in the white tiled arena it sits in..

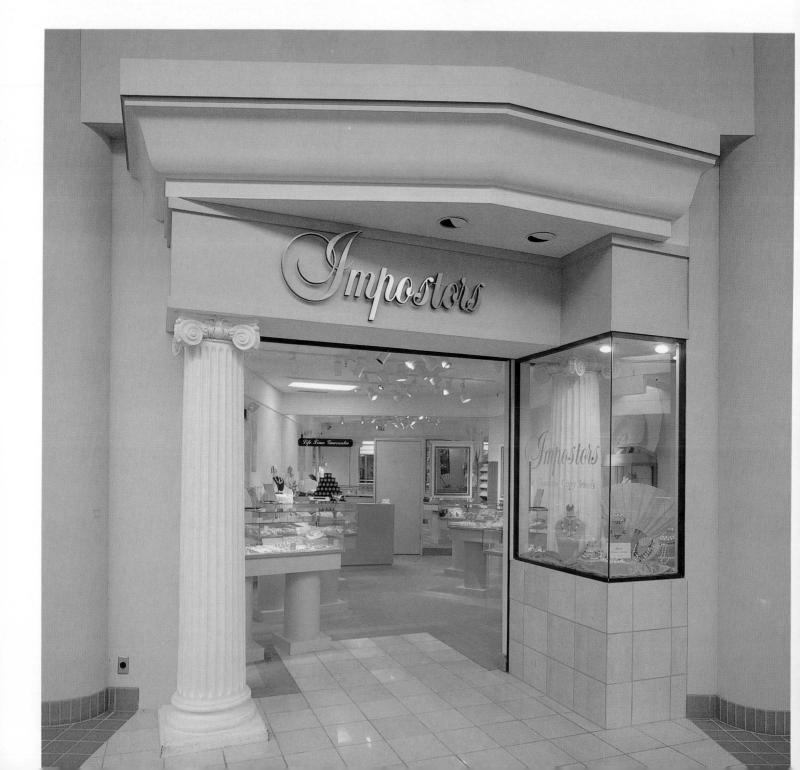

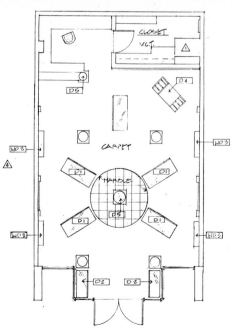

D'MAR JEWELRY

Plaza Bahia, Acapulco, Gro., Mexico

Design:
FERNANDO LEON
ESCALANTE &
JOSE LOPEZ CRISTIANI
MEXICO CITY, MEXICO

The light green and turquoise color scheme that is used fills the shop with an irridescent shimmer reminiscent of an underwater world, — and the "sea" in the store's name. The faceted mirrored entrance element, and the cut and angled lines in the interior were meant to create the sensation of being inside a gem. The multi-angled floor pattern and the pyramid ceiling above reiterate the "faceted gem" motif. The ambient lighting is contained in the stepped ceiling, while low voltage lamps add sparkle to the mirrored niches inside the shop.

130

HERMES Union Square, San Francisco, CA

Project Architect:
RINA DUMAS
ARCHITECTURE
INTERIEURE, PARIS
Design Team:
CHRISTOPHE KUNTZ /
JOSEPHINA D.L. RICHEZ

Coordinating Architect:
WHISLER-PATRI
SAN FRANCISCO
Project Manager:
KEVIN DILL, AIA
Lighting Consultant:
DOUGLAS BAKER, NY

Cabinetry:
FINK & SCHINDLER
Photographer:
NORMAN MC GRATH

This dramatic store that faces onto Union Square not only echoes the famed store on the Rue St. Honore in Paris, it is also the largest Hermes store in the United States. The 3100 sq. ft. of retail space includes the main selling floor which is filled with fashion accessories like scarves, belts, bags and small leather goods. This main entry level gradually steps up towards the rear of the store in a series of selling plateaus. The forced perspective of the design draws the shopper to the grand staircase and the sculpture created by French artist Christian Renonciat. The brass railings, the planked cherrywood floor edged with French limestone, the frosted "grecque" lights (an Hermes "signature"), and the handsome, custom designed, cherrywood cases all add up to the "understated elegance" that is Hermes.

At the top of the stairs, on the second floor, a jewelry salon and houseware boutique greet the shopper. A hallway, lined in saddles and accessories, leads to the light filled, ready-to-wear area which overlooks the palm trees on Union Square. The interiors of the cases are lit with custom designed fluorescents to enhance the texture of the leathers. Halogens have been matched with the incandescent lights that are strategically placed in the ceiling, — all in harmony with the illuminated frosted "grecques" chandeliers that are so characteristic of the Paris decor. Altogether the lighting creates an enchanting ambience in a design already rich in ambience. Mme. Dumas said, "It gives me a special pleasure to be able to suggest in an abstract fashion the hills of San Francisco while at the same time introducing innovative structural techniques and creative merchandising fixtures, making the reality of shopping more gracious for Hermes patrons."

THE COACH STORE

Westfarm, CT

Architect & Designer:
   ROSENBLUM-HARB,
   ARCHITECTS, NY
Principal:
   ELLIOTT ROSENBLUM

Job Captain:
   ARON PORTNOY
Illustration:
   LIDIA HERES
Photographer:
   ROBERT MILLER

Recently renovated, this 1200 sq. ft. space now truly represents the fine, "traditional" and classic quality that upscale customers have come to associate with the Coach name. The store's facade, as well as the interior, is faced with rift sawn oak that has been stained a deep red/brown, and detailed with mouldings, panels and cannellated pilasters. The interior has the atmosphere of a lovely, old country-English library, and the feeling is enhanced by the gliding stepladder that leads up to the top shelf, and the deep, dramatic cornice mouldings above. The cash/wrap counter is topped with marble and the central bow is echoed in the arched area on the rear wall.

LUCHESE BOOT STORE San Antonio, TX

Design:
WHITFIELD & CHOATE
NASHVILLE, TN

Creative Director/Interior Designer:
BRAD WHITFIELD

Design Associate:
JIM HSIEH

"Only a store with museum quality appointments and decor would be good enough to present the heritage and craftsmanship of Lucchese Boots," and that is what the client got when the designer created this unique setting for the quality product. The ceiling is cypress beamed and surfaced with stucco, as are the hand screened walls. The bare floor is made of hand-finished, wide planked walnut overlaid with fine area rugs that were dyed to match a piece of Anasazi pottery. All the custom furniture is crafted of walnut and the "bar" is inlaid with ebony, ivory, turquoise and abalone mother-of-pearl. A variety of museum-quality Western relics and artifacts were assembled and lovingly displayed under the recessed incandescent lamps. The residential/museum setting serves the aesthetics of the product.

MARTINEZ VALERO

Third Ave., NYC

Design:
  ARCUS DESIGN GROUP, NY
Special Fixtures:
  PELL ARTIFEX
MILARI FURNITURE
PETER SLEP CABINETS

The 1600 sq. ft. of space in this prototype design for a Spanish manufacturer of fine ladies shoes, is divided on two levels — and provides for show and storage. The design concept: "A modern interpretation of the historical connotations and classical elegance inherent in the new Spain." A monolithic Duquesa Rosa marble triptych is set in the corner window with the inlaid, gold-leafed, logo, and serves as signage and a setting for the shoe displays. Inside, rich materials in bold forms create a series of receding focal points. The tinted plaster surfaces (Art-In Construction) serve as a background for floating glass shelves. In the center of the shop, under a gold-leafed vault, a display fixture made of honey onyx cradled in verdegris patina capped bronze towers (Pell-Artifex). Platinum Birds-Eye Maple veneer and curved glass are used in the free standing cabinets and the cash/wrap desk.

JOAN & DAVID
South Coast Plaza, Costa Mesa, CA

Design:
EVA JIRICNA ARCHITECTS
Project Architect:
JON TOLLIT

Design Team:
EVA JIRICNA
DUNCAN WEBSTER, C.J. LIM
U.S. Consultant Architect:
CHATTERTON JEZEK
PARTNERSHIP, L.A.

Staircase & Balustrade:
MARSHALL HOWARD
Furniture:
MATTHEW MARCHBANK
with STEELCASE

The multiangled, soaring, two storey walls of glass open up all of the Joan & David shop to the mall shopper. It is space incarnate, and connecting the blacked out second level, where the stock is kept, from the glowing white selling level is the fabulous, fantasy staircase that is more than just the link, — it is a theatrical extravaganza — and experience in flight. The "staircase," as a design element, is a Jiricna trademark, and one of her designs is sure to add spectacle to any store's selling space. The staircase is a combination of stainless steel balustrading and laminated glass treads. Since shoes are usually difficult to display with style,

Jiricna developed translucent, laminated glass shelves suspended, at an angle, from cables which are attached to decorative but holding chromed clamps. All units are backlit. The color palette is mostly black and white with a deep regal red stain on the wood of the curved displayer units. The red is also used to accent the black leather tufted benches (*see left*). The black granite floors provide a perimeter of reflecting surface for the sparkling displays, and softer, warmer carpeting is used around the central seating area. A floating, suspended plaster ceiling is hung over the central space and it is redefined by the gallery around the second level.

GOLDI

900 N. Michigan, Chicago, IL

Design:
   KUBALA/WASKATKO,
   ARCHITCTS, INC.,
   CEDARBURG, WI

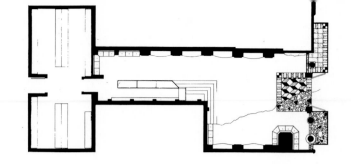

Located in the Bloomingdale's Atrium building, in 1240 sq. ft. of space, is this fascinating shoe shop that, from its unique "schizoid" exterior, tells shoppers that this is a store "on the cutting edge of fashion and design." The client wanted an environment that would "bombard the senses" and that is what he got in this store which exuberantly mixes Memphis-style colored motifs with the Italian Renaissance as typified in the ceiling of the Sistine Chapel. Arching over the entire store is a classic barrel vault with a painted Venus attended by cherubs ascending in a vortex of clouds down to the classic architecture on the right side of the store. Here, the dressy shoes are elegantly displayed in corbelled and pedimented niches. On the other half of the store, the more casual shoes are colorfully presented in Memphisian shadow boxes. The flooring is a melange of black/white tiles, zebra stripes and paisley-patterned designs. Plaster cherubs, stuffed pigeons, faux finishes, zolotoned surfaces, reflecting mirrors and an excellent lighting plan — together — create a memorable store that is anything but boring.

CABLE & CO.

London, England

Design:
DDA, DAVID DAVIS
ASSOCIATES,
LONDON, ENGLAND

Cable & Co. is the British Shoe Corporation's new shoe retailing concept aimed at the young, fashion conscious consumer. The interior design is in a "traditional English style" — fresh and uncluttered, and enriched with cherrywood panelling and fixtures. Cherrywood is also used for the consoles along the walls under the wooden shell system that is used to present a display of the merchandise. Customer seating is on long benches on a deep green carpet that is bordered by the stone floor. The displays are lit by low voltage spots, and the general illumination is from the specially designed glass and copper pendant lights. Up front, — at the entrance, there are the traditional English "niceties"; an umbrella stand and even a wrought iron shoe scraper outside. DDA was also responsible for all elements of graphics and packaging including quality wrapping paper, shoe boxes, and bags. This is the flagship of the new group and nine additional stores are in the works.

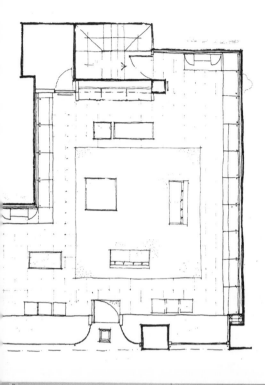

HAHN SHOES

Tysons Corner Center, McLean, VA

Store Design:
    BILL STAFFORD,
    HAHN SHOES
Architecture:
    THE ARCHITECTURE GROUP,
    BATON ROUGE, LA
    SAMMY VINCENT

Fixturing:
    ABSTRACTS, VAN NUYS, CA
    JK CABINETS,
    BALTIMORE, MD
Photographer:
    MAXWELL MAC KENZIE,
    WASHINGTON, DC

Hahn is a multi-line, shoe chain of about 80 outlets located mainly on the east coast — ranging from Rhode Island to Florida. The Hahn name has been associated with shoes, in the Washington area, since 1876. Though the shoes are market positioned as "moderate priced footwear," management felt an upgraded store image was in order so that Hahn could stant out from the crowd of shoe stores in a given mall. That new image was realized with the contemporary/classic look that appeared in the recently renovated and up-graded Tysons Corner Center. Since this mall is located in the company's home base, Washington, DC, — "we feel that the store expresses a certain monumentality and permanence that we think is indicative of our position in this market area." In other areas, the designers will make reference to the unique architectural heritage of the particular area. The pediment and columns motif that creates the entrance arch into the shop is reiterated in the window fixtures and on the selling floor. A "Jefferson Memorial" circular colonnade makes a dramatic focal point in the center of the shop, — flanked by Corinthian capped, mirror-covered columns.

TIP TOE

Cumberland Mall, Atlanta, GA

Design:
   DESIGN FORUM,
   DAYTON, OH
Principal:
   LEE CARPENTER
Design Director:
   BILL CHIDLEY
Project Manager:
   GREG LAPP
Lighting Design:
   STEVE BRAZIER
Photographer:
   ANDY SNOW

The Butler Company realized that they were missing a segment in the fashion accessory area. The gap in the market was a shoe store that focused in on the young, fad-fashionable, 15 to 25 year old shopper who was up-scale in attitude but also value conscious. To fill this area, Tip Top was created and the designers's task was to promote a high level of brand awareness, in an atmosphere that would quickly, — and easily, — shift with trends in fashion. That environment needed to be modular, easy and fast to changeover or roll-out, and "communicate" with the target market out in the mall. The store is light, — neutral in color and rich in colored graphics, and sparkling with pulsating neon lines and incandescent light. The industrial approach is evident in devices like the steel roller conveyors full of colorful shoe boxes, the wave-like shelves, wheeled carts and black tubular fixturing. This prototype was selected as a Store of the Year by Chain Store Age Executives.

TOP'N'KNOT

Newport Centre, Jersey City, NJ

Design:
    THE INTERNATIONAL
    DESIGN GROUP, USA, INC.,
    NY
Project Director:
    KEITH KOVAR
Senior Designer:
    COLLETTE
Photographer:
    SCOTT FRANCES

In a strange, angled space of less than 800 sq. ft., in a new mall just across from Manhattan, this new concept store has appeared. The name says it all; the store carries hats and ties and things that knot — for women and men. The facade is a glass "greenhouse" enclosure full of vertical and diagonal planes, and the neon illuminated sign marks the actual store entrance. The space within is broken up with sharply angled, gray slatwall dividers upon which are stocked soft hats in white wire mesh baskets. Off white columns, capped with large milk-glass, globe lights become a "forest of hat trees" with more hats projecting off of giant pins. The jutting angles of the dividers and the thrust of the cash/wrap counter keep the shopper moving in and around the columns, and get her/him into the far end of the store. Behind the cash/wrap unit, a handsome display of ties for the shoppers' perusal and approval. This store was honored in the recent NRMA/ISP store design contest.

FLORIS

Madison Ave., NYC

Design:
  WALKER GROUP/CNI, NY
Project Executive/Designer:
  GARRY K. VAN PATTER
Director of Graphics:
  PETER SCAUVZZO

Project Executive:
  BILL WICHART
Graphic Design:
  LISA KENTONICKAS
Designer:
  TRINA CARLSON

After 250 successful years on Jermyn Street in London, Floris has expanded into the U.S. with this small and traditional shop on Madison Avenue. The designers have been able to reflect the history, quality and refinement of the original Floris, yet adapt it all to satisfy the self-service merchandising methods appropriate for the American market. The design includes "signature" images and details of the historic, original store such as the patterned carpets, arched top wall cases and fine wood cases and counters. All these elements have been refined into a "kit of parts" which will facilitate laying out and installing future roll-out sites.

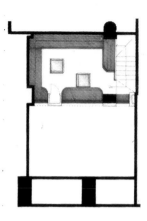
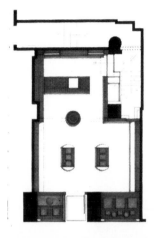

CHILDREN

No where is the battle between the "hungry" retailer and the "design for design's sake" store planner more evident than in Children's clothing stores. The merchandise is bright and colorful and often so are the selling spaces. The retailer jams the store full of merchandise and the designer trowels on cute gimmicks and decoratives that are supposed to enhance the garments but usually ends up in a clash of colors — and wills.

A well designed Children's store is truly a treasure — and a pleasure, and we were delighted to find some excellent examples of well thought out stores. In our selections we do see a meeting of the minds and talents of the retailer and the designer. We see what can result when the designer acknowledges the retailer's needs and stocking requirements, and when the retailer respects the designer's solution to the problem and follows the agreed upon visual merchandising techniques.

Visual Merchandising is always a vital element in good store design. In a Children's store it is a must and may in many ways determine architectural solutions, and fixture layout in the retail space. The merchandise is small in scale, often strong in color and pattern, and overwhelming in size variety. First and foremost, the merchandise must be arranged in a neat, orderly, cohesive and comprehensible manner. It must appeal to the mother or adult shopper as well as the child who is about to be inveigled into the try-on session. The ambience must provide a relaxing and calming quality that takes the chore out of the selection process and makes it a pleasurable experience for the fitter and the fit-upon. For some adults, shopping is a treat; for children it is rarely an event to look forward to with anticipation. When both parent and child can wander through bright, open spaces, — see merchandise on easy-to-select and easy-to-co-ordinate fixtures, —

under happy, sparkling light, — feel unhindered and uninhibited, — actually free to move and touch, the designer has done a successful store.

Following are some successful store designs. We have not, because of space, done full justice to the many excellent "Children's World" that are appearing in more and more department stores across the country. In these friendly, spacious areas, the parent and the child are treated with excellent visual merchandising, accentuated and underscored with top, in-store, on-the-floor, display vignettes that not only show the newest merchandise coordinated, — they also underline the scale of the shop and make the child feel more at ease, and in proportion, to the new environment. The child can relate to the child size mannequins or soft sculpture figures, and the activities they are involved in. The child is often in touch — on the same level — with the kids on display.

In children's wear shops there are also a variety of markets and attitudes and we are showing several in this chapter. Pepperino is an up-scale, urban, sophisticated shop for Yuppie parents and doting grandparents who usually buy their own clothes on Madison Ave. McKids is a new store and a new concept, from the Sears organization, for a popular priced shop where the style and smartness of the fixturing also becomes the decor of the sales space. Kids 'N' Action combines some children's wear with sportswear and toys in a gentle, old-fashioned town setting. In the smallest of mall spaces, Bubblegummers has created a carefree shop for children's wear, shoes and go-with accessories, — all on display and beautifully controlled by the visual merchandising established by wall and floor fixtures.

Good design can make shopping also fun for most children, — and their parents.

Left: Strawbridge & Clothier, King of Prussia, PA
Design: Pavlik Design Team, Ft. Lauderdale, FL
For Strawbridge & Clothier: John Witmeyer, Dir
of V.M. Design

MC KIDS

Brickyard Mall, Chicago, IL

Design:
   NEIDERMAIER, CHICAGO

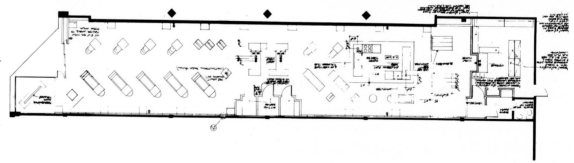

Sears Roebuck and Co., — with a license from McDonalds, has come up with a new, free-standing children's store designed from a child's eye perspective. The store combines clothing, shoes, accessories, toys, games, books, and fun novelties for the child from birth up to age ten. The store also features educational, interactive and creative activities for the children who can enter into the store through their own, child-size door. In the light, bright-white interior, the kids are free to wander and touch the within reach merchandise while they are entertained by the over-scaled, dimensional toys and decoratives. The lighting is clear and fresh and intensifies the sharp colors of the merchandise and the displays.

KIDS 'N' ACTION

Stonebridge Mall, Pleasanton, CA

Design:
GENSLER & ASSOCIATES,
SAN FRANCISCO, CA
Project Director:
CHARLES KRIDLER
Design Director:
RONETTE KING

Design Team:
LAURA DUNSFORD
WARNER WONG
KUEI-TING YANG
JOHN BRICKER
TOM HORTON

Artist:
LAURIE LAMBERTSON
Photographer:
SHARON RISEDORPH
SAN FRANCISCO

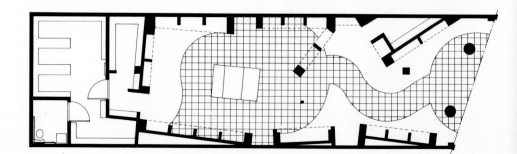

This 1300 sq. ft. shop is a prize winning prototype for a child's activity toy store. The children are encouraged to touch and to play with the merchandise, and the parents are "encouraged" to enter and walk through the extra wide aisles that accommodate strollers — and the toy-testers. The concept is a "toy village," and the entry into the "town" is through the ribbon swirled facade (right) and on to the "road" simulated with the flooring material. The town consists of six, eight foot tall architectural facades that represent a variety of community buildings. Each houses a special category of merchandise, like the dancewear in the Ballet School Building. The facades are set off at different angles to provide interest, create a traffic pattern and also provide stock storage space behind the facades. A lemonade stand serves as the cash/wrap desk. All the colors are white or pastel to not conflict with the mainly primary colors of the merchandise.

GYMBOREE

Valley Fair, San Jose, CA

Design:
STORE PLANNER
ASSOCIATES
SANTA CLARA, CA
Designer:
DON LIPP

Gymboree provides "environment for the total child" — wear, gear and equipment. What started out as a play and exercise program for children has blossomed into a retail setting for "Yuppie looking kidswear, videos, books, building blocks, and toy musical instruments. Children are invited to play — to touch — to enjoy themselves in the child-proofed, 1000 sq. ft. space that has a pine wood floor with gym markings, — surrounded by natural wood, child-scaled fixtures

and bright, primary colored laminated surfaces. The entrance is an arch of giant, colored blocks and the Gymboree logo is multicolored and lilting. Inside, the red metal hang-lights come down to warm up the already red-enriched surfaces. Dolls wear the Gymboree clothes and provide a sense of fun and serve as display elements on the floor fixtures and above the fascia that outlines the perimeter walls — and "brings down" the ceiling.

BUBBLEGUMMERS

Concepcion, Chile

Design:
    MARIA A. LISOWICZ

This relatively small, 600 sq. ft., shop is part of the worldwide chain of shoe stores owned and operated by the Bata Shoe organization. In this new specialty store Bata has addressed the large segment of consumers in the medium-to-high income bracket, that have till now not found the specific type of children's footwear they want in the traditional Bata Family shoe shore. A Bubblegummers shop rarely exceeds 700 sq. ft. in size, and it is sometimes a part of — and still apart from —

a traditional Family store. The design concept is simple and is based on colorful building blocks; geometric shapes in modular sizes that offer a multitude of design opportunities. Red enameled metal tube fixtures on the wall complement the ceiling grid that holds the sharp accent lights. In addition to the shoes, there is a selection of clothes, accessories and toys, — all contained within the soft colored interior.

PEPPERINO

Third Ave., NY

Design:
 ZB INC., NY
Principals:
 FREDERIC M. ZONSIUS &
 LORI BEITLER
Photographer:
 DURSTON SAYLOR

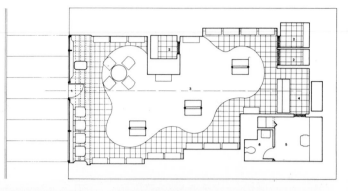

On a busy commercial street, this store is almost within touching distance of Bloomingdale's, — and the Bloomingdale-type of up-scaled shopper. The store carries high fashion children's wear and caters, in its slick 1560 sq. ft. of space, to the contemporary, "with-it," mother. An amoeba shaped, patterned area rug centers the store, and it floats on the terrazzo tiled floor. Vertically panelled walls reach up to the dropped, gray ceiling that carries the tracks of low voltage, tungsten lamps. Lifesized, soft sculptured kids people the shop serving, humorously, as show-offs for the featured merchandise. Simple and effective slotted systems, on the walls, carry the stacked and hung garments.

HOME FASHIONS

Stores and departments specializing in "Linens" and "Home Furnishings" are almost as dated and passe as are "White Sales" that prominently feature neat piles of ribbon tied sheets and pillow cases being presented by "French Maids" in abbreviated black skirts and showing layers of white ruffled petticoats. Linens are still being stacked by color, but there are many more colors, — and patterns, to separate or coordinate, — to arrange or juxtapose, for new interest. There are also designers who get top billing; interior designers, architects, stylists and, probably, most important, — the couture designers who have expanded their scope, — come off the fashion runway and gone into the bedroom, the bath, kitchen and even the closet. These fashion designers and interior designers are creating signature groupings in exciting fashion colors and patterns. Home Furnishings is now Home Fashions, and once again Americans are returning to the home and the "in" concept for the Nineties is Cocooning.

Many men and women left their homes to work in the marketplace and now there appears to be a return to the home for a workspace. With the tremendous advances in electronics, in computers, in telephone hook-ups and with everybody fax-ing, it is more than just possible for more of the work force to work in and from the home. The development of newer and better — and bigger forms of home entertainment has made "staying in" a favorite evening pastime for many who formerly had to go out. With so much emphasis on the home for day and evening occupation and recreation, Home Fashions has become the big, expanding area in retailing for the '90s.

In this chapter we have included some of the new directions retailers and their store designers are taking in bringing home and fashion together into an indivisible entity. In every instance, display is a major consideration in the store's design. No longer is it "show"; now it is "presentation." Color stacking is not the whole answer; color and pattern coordination and accessorizing is vital. The retailer doesn't just show a couch or a table or a chair; the retailer presents a visually designed and well lit vignette setting or even a model room setting that includes the furniture, the right wall, floor and window treatments, the assorted accessories and even the correct magazine casually left open — on the table. It is all life-style design and its identification for the shopper. As in menswear and womenswear, where the costumes are provided so the actors and actresses can dress for the parts they play in their day-to-day, real-life, soap operas, so the retailer of home fashions provides the stage settings upon which the action can take place. Combined with the emphasis on the time spent in the home and the home being a visible extension of who and what one is, — well, it is big business!

Our selections have been mainly limited to specialty stores, but we feel it is imperative that we mention the "World of Home Fashion" now in orbit in major department stores. We have shown a single department store which exemplifies what is going on where the department has become a "department store-within-the-department store." They are often a collection of specialty stores and designer boutiques. The professional displays tell the stories, separate or combine various classifications, and create the bigger sale. Here, the shopper can find a great, in-depth selection of many coordinated pieces of merchandise.

Yes, Cocooning is "in" — and it is "in" in style — and fashion.

Left: Giles & Co., New York, NY
Modern Stone Age, Greene St., Soho, NY
Design: Jean Jacques Ferron & Francois Vallee

GILES & CO. Columbus Ave., NYC

Design:
    MOJO/STUMER
    ARCHITECTS,
    GREAT NECK, NY

Architect/Prinipal in Charge:
    MARK D. STUMER, RA
Project Designer:
    ANDREW WYNNYK
Project Manager:
    MIKE DOYLE

Staff:
    PAUL SEDGLEY,
    PROJECT ARCHITECT
    WENDY BLUMSTEIN,
    INTERIORS

7500 sq. ft. of what was once a restaurant in a venerable old Hotel was converted into a multi-level, exciting retail facility for showing and selling furniture and fine home accessories. The designers created a circulation program that carries the shopper through all areas of the store and to the large furniture area in the rear. This area is defined by a large contemporary trellis that contains the space under a barrel vaulted skylight that lets in the daylight. Display cabinets are set up as major design elements and are also departmentalized. In addition to the natural light there is a generous supply of spots and uplights.

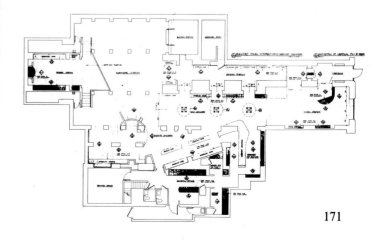

171

THE SHAPES OF DESIGN

Westwood, Los Angeles, CA

Design:
INTERIOR SPACES, INC.,
VENICE, CA
Principal/Designers:
SHARI CANEPA, ASID

Project Designer:
LISA SIEGMAN, ASID
Lighting Consultant:
DELTA WHOLESALE
LIGHTING

Photographer:
NICK SPRINGETT

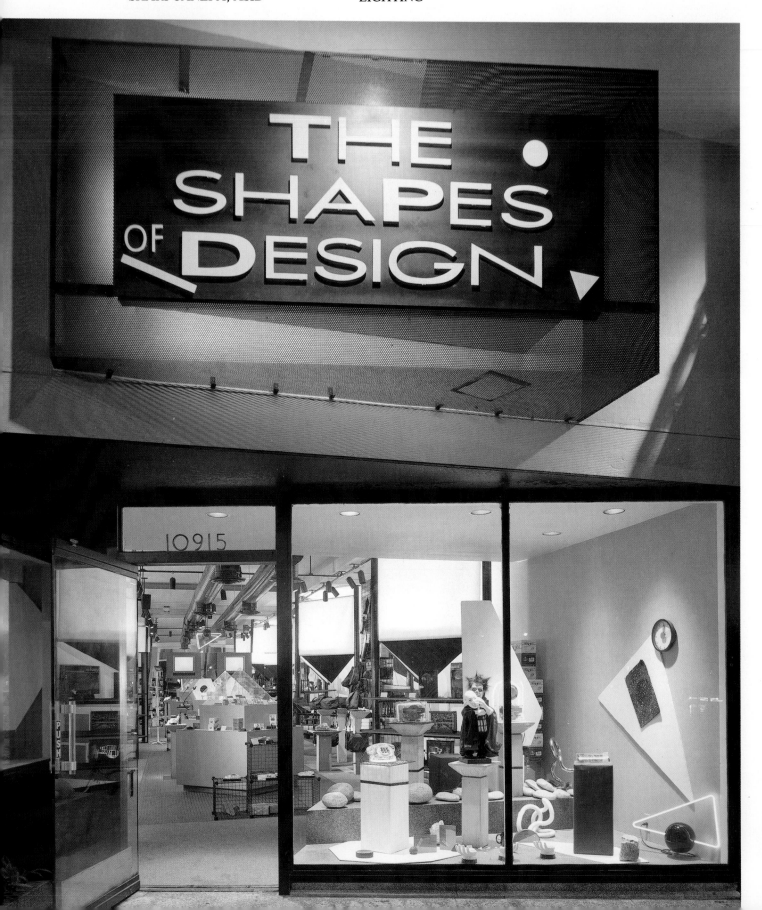

The main facade detail is the perforated metal wedge that projects off the flat fascia and carries the store's name — and introduces the triangle. The key to the design of the 720 sq. ft. space is the triangle as it is used in the black wooden shields that hide the ordinary fluorescent lamps hung above each group of shelves on the angled perimeter walls. The tubes can be geled over to change the color of the area and thus keep the store changing in color to go with the changes in products.

The triangle is used in the vertical and horizontal planes as well as in the lucite pyramids that contain small items on the floor displayers. The palette is neutral, — gray and black, and the designers were constrained by a tight budget, and thus had to improvise with elements that were left by the previous tenant. An example: Using the floor-to-ceiling posts that originally held hang rods to become the dividing element in the design.

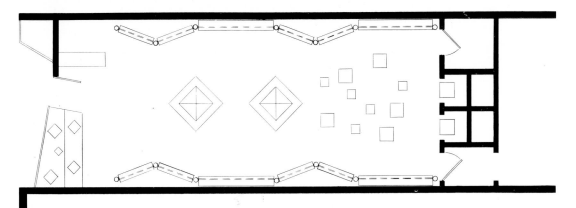

THE LIGHT SOURCE Columbus, OH

Design:
RICHARDSONSMITH,
WORTHINGTON, OH

Design Team:
KEVIN COLANDER
BETH DORSEY
DAN DORSEY
SUSAN HALLER
SANDY MC KISSICK
KELLY MOONEY
PAUL WESTRICK

Architect:
JAMES F. RILEY
Light Engineers:
LARSON ENGINEERING

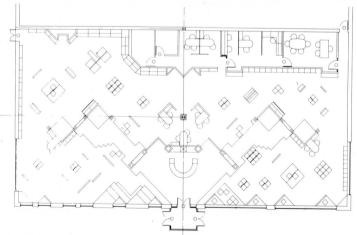

"We found that lighting stores were all doing the same things," said Lance Vetter of the Elgee Electric Supply Co., — the parent company of this new store/showroom, "and the customers were intimidated by the amount of product displayed and the lack of information available." Thus, the designers came up with the "home environment" concept and the various departments are laid out following the logical flow of a home floor plan. There are "thresholds" that architecturally define the path and create visual milestones for the customer. The ceiling plane, in the departments, is tiered to accommodate an assortment of related lighting products. Display vignettes support these areas and feature life-style furnishings and decorative accessories.

LIGHT TALK

BAJOS

Plaza Bahia, Acapulco, Gro. Mexico

Design:
FERNANDO LEON
ESCALANTE &
JOSE LOPEZ CRISTIANI
Photographer:
ANTONIO PEDROZA

A wave of the future for the electronic and computerized home of today. Undulating curves take over the dynamic ceiling design and move the shoppers through the multi-arced selling space. Dramatic color is used with the wave-like motif and the merchandise is set out within reach of the shopper — to handle and to manipulate.

Design:
**ACE ARCHITECTS,
OAKLAND, CA**
Photographer:
ROB SUPER

CACHIBACHI

Berkley, CA

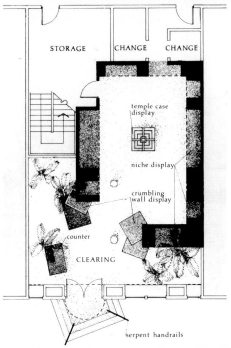

To house an exotic collection of unusual objet d'art and home accessories, the designers attempted to create a place "overtaken by time and foliage" in the 1250 sq. ft. of space. There are "tall stone walls rent apart, and thick vines that clutch at space apparently once sacred, while artifacts, betraying a primitive culture, rest alongside and atop the ruins." The shoppers are invited to explore Cachibachi for treasures — and pleasures.

177

BAZAR BAHIA

Plaza Bahia, Acapulco, Gro., Mexico

Design:
FERNANDO LEON
ESCALANTE &
JOSE LOPEZ CRISTIANI,
MEXICO CITY, MEXICO
Photographer:
ANTONIO PEDROZA

The arts and crafts shop is Mexican in concept, — in color, — in texture and in architectural details, — all smartly contemporized. There are influences of the Aztecs with pyramids appearing and encrusted niches serving as display showcases. The clay tiled floor is accented with natural wood grooves and the dropped ceilings form vaulted areas which are washed with indirect light. The textured walls are colored sienna, ocher, orange and earthy brown to create visual bays and areas within the shop.

WATERFORD WEDGWOOD

Manhasset, NY

Design:
NEAL STEWART /
DESIGN ASSOCIATES,
DALLAS, TX

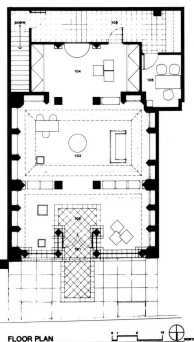

"Waterford Wedgwood exemplifies timeless style and elegance worldwide" and needed a setting that would express and house the faithfully reproduced, century-old patterns and at the same time reflect the vibrant corporate Waterford Wedgwood of today." A merger was effected, by the designer, by employing in a rather contemporary manner, traditional architectural details like columns, base and cornice mouldings, marbles and wood. That design concept begins on the exterior of the shop and is continued within. The simple squared marble column on a plinth is repeated, as a motif, inside the store like part of a colonnade. The simple marble sign completes the facade and says "status."

FLOOR PLAN

181

Within, high gloss, white lacquered columns are contrasted with Canadian Maple wood, and the Wedgwood blue that was made famous centuries ago in England. To complement the fixed perimeter fixtures, the designer devised a series of free-standing "forward" fixtures, — adaptable to seasonal and special product displays. Following the structural grid, a rhythmic pattern of three bays was evolved which incorporates columns and pilasters. Along the side walls, smaller bays or display cabinets are used to hold the china and

glass on the glass shelves. Low voltage, halogen lighting was unobstrusively integrated into the display cabinets, and undershelf lighting strips shine through the clear shelves, — bouncing off the mirrored sides and the base shelf. Wool back panel fabrics were custom dyed to a color that would best complement the brilliant lead crystal and translucent bone china. As visible, right, all details and shapes were chosen to enhance the circular china and crisp crystal profiles.

IN DETAIL

Whiteflint Mall, Bethesda, MD

Design:
  JACOBS & PRATT, INC., NY

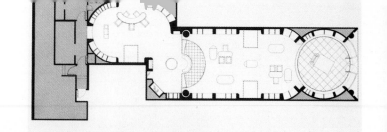

The bold sweep of the fascia proudly introduces, in gold Roman letter, In Detail, — a new retail concept shop of the J.C. Penney Co. By itself, in an up-scaled mall, it makes a strong, dramatic statement and the shop is on view through the curved glass front and the gracious wide entranceway. The Baroque sweep of the facade is repeated in the rose colored marble outlining and accentuating the circular arena — front and center — where a bed is made up in the best and latest of bed linens and accessories. As visible in the plan, the arc is repeated throughout the store's layout and suggests intimacy and femininity. Softly curved mahogany walls encompass the marble stage and they are, in turn, beautifully merchandised with linens and bed and bath accessories.

Complementary brass and mahogany wood carts and
gondolas were custom designed to provide presentation
flexibility for ever-changing collections on the floor.
The voluptuous bull-nosed moldings, rounded ends and
arced uprights reiterate the prominent curves of the
facade and entrance walls. The floor displays are
illuminated by low voltage lamps while recessed
incandescents cast light down onto the peach flooring
which is a major part of the color scheme of the
interior — with the mahogany and the warm light.
Above: Two consultant stations on the selling floor to
personalize the shopping experience and provide the
service that should accompany luxury items.

KRIS KELLEY
Union Square, San Francisco, CA

Design:
MEDIA FIVE LTD.
COSTA MESA, CA
Project Director & Designer/Architect:
THOMAS R. PUGLIUSO, AIA
OF THOS. PUGLIUSO
DESIGN ASSOC.
Project Manager:
HENRY G. WONG, AIA
Photographer:
CHARLES MC GRATH
SAN FRANCISCO

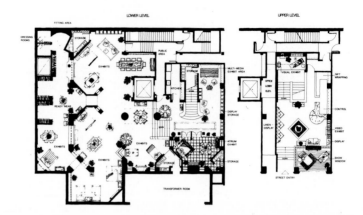

Kris Kelley is a linen showroom that debuted in the retail field with this first shop. It was imperative that the designers create an image — and an identity — that would represent the owners' conception of their service, merchandising and persona. "Kris Kelley is a collage of places, times and spaces," located in approximately 6000 sq. ft. of usable space — on three levels; 1200 sq. ft. on the ground level and 4800 on an adjacent level below. A rubble rock wall extends from the entry door to the rear display area and imbues the space with a sense of antiquity. Three sandblasted trusses traversely span the length of the level and the verde, blue-green, marble of the entry landing gives way to the white washed, white oak strip flooring.

188

Wall sconces, downlights, track lighting and specialty lighting on programmable switches provides flexibility to preset up to four different lighting scenes or moods. The first level down is "resplendent with a fireplace, limestone mantle and hearth, arched passages, sandblasted wood beams and high intensity lighting." On the lowest level (pictured right) different areas are divided and separated by walls with windowed openings, arched wall sections and assorted ceiling planes. The flooring is oak throughout and thus connects all spaces and display vignettes with each vignette creating its own sense of place and time. Custom designed shelves, on the perimeter walls, meet specific packaging requirements. "Kris Kelley creates a comfortable atmosphere which provides an ease and graciousness for seeing linens displayed in a variety of evocative and romantic ways."

SCARBOROUGH

Queens Quay Terminal, Toronto, Ont., Canada

Design:
THE INTERNATIONAL
DESIGN GROUP, TORONTO
Executive Vice President:
R. MAC LACHLIN
Architect/Designer:
NELLA FIORINO /
PAULIS CISKEVICIUS

In a relatively small space, 750 sq. ft., — in a rehabbed terminal-turned-mall, the designers, in turn, converted indoor space into an outdoor space. The result is a theatrical, storybook garden setting influenced and dominated by the delicate cross banding and lattice-work of the Chinese Chippendale designs. Cool green lacquered fixtures were created to incorporate the lattice design, geometric elements, — and also complement the airiness of the architectural frames.

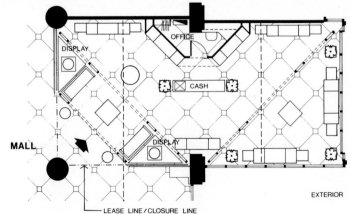

EXTERIOR

LEASE LINE/CLOSURE LINE

The store plan is based on opposing 45 degree angled, post and beam constructed architectural frames which define the entrance and also alleviates the space of its recillinear format. White antique bird baths overflow with potpourri, up front, at the entrance. The gazebo with balcony above becomes the anchor for the space and contains the office and stockroom. Tromp l'oeil artwork on the door to the offices is repeated on the walls over the architectural shelf units, and it is carried through to an airbrushed blue sky with floating clouds on the ceiling. The latticework planterboxes with trees reinforce the elements of nature — and the outdoors theme of the design.

MARSHALL FIELD

Galleria, Houston, TX

Design:
   TSR, TUCCI
   SEGRETE ROSEN, NY

In a "world" of its own in the new Marshall Field department store, in Houston is Home Fashions. Located on the top level and capping the "townhouse" concept of the designers, the department evolves off the open atrium with a wood tiled aisle that leads around the area. In the "Euro-style" feeling, there is natural wood lined walls and partitions that are capped with classically inspired, deep crown mouldings, also paneled details that increase the residential quality of the setting.

Designer shops, like the Ralph Lauren Collection, above, are treated as skeletal enclosures that lend an extra sense of prestige to the products contained within. Fluorescent luminaires are combined with incandescent spots to create a "home" environment while featured merchandise is glowingly presented in co-ordinated displays. On the same level, the Kitchen shops are bright, light and white with stuccoed walls and columns of marble and glass.

LEISURE-LIFE

This chapter is a potpourri; a mixture, a melange, a compilation of bits and pieces of the retail scene that aren't quite "fashion" but must still be "fashionable." The shoppers that frequent these stores are the same shoppers who shop designer boutiques and brand-name shops in up-scaled malls and on fashion worthy streets. These stores are also specialty shops and the shoppers are the worldly, upwardly mobile men and women who are life-style oriented, but — most important — these shops are for the free-time in their lives.

This is where shoppers can indulge in their fantasies — spend time and money on the little, often superficial, things that make life more meaningful — richer and fuller. Here, time does not count and money doesn't either, the shopper satisfies his/her ego in a toy-shop for grown-ups. Whether it is selecting the just-right running shoes, or the perfect stereo equipment, the status car phone, or the smooth and silk stationery, — there is no rush because this is not a chore, — it is a pleasure. With the ever-increasing interest in health and keeping the body in shape, the sports-oriented stores have grown in importance and have been forced to "departmentalize" or "specialize." Now it is Home Fitness Shops as well as Active Sportswear shops, and there are even those stores that will dress you as a participant or as an observer for spor-

ting events. A pair of sneakers is more than rubber, leather or canvas. Sneakers make a statement about the shopper's life-style, — about who he is, what he does and even tells you where he does it. The snacks we select and where we select them is also part of the individual's image profile. Does he eat junk food? Does she pick the healthy, diet aware fruit and nut bar? This is not like doing the weekly shopping; this is instant and very person gratification.

Thus, our shops are up-scaled shops done with style, attractive, inviting and comfortable enough to keep the shopper there for a long time without once referring to his watch. As in any retail shop that caters to those who are knowledgable and selective, the visual merchandising is as important as the overall ambience that contains the merchandise. The setting can often make the item appear more desirable; it can stroke the ego of the pampered patron and also provide the framework for the daydream fulfillment.

That is what this Leisure-Life chapter is all about; for the TIME in YOUR life. Not the necessities but the niceties — the everyday "luxuries" that make us feel special to ourselves. Not the clothes that dress the body but the layerings onto the spirit that make our free time very special time.

Left: Sports Unlimited, Plymouth Meeting, PA

SPORTS UNLIMITED

Plymouth Meeting Mall, Plymouth Meeting, PA

Design:
   BANIK/CUMBY, INC.
   SWARTHMORE, PA
Project Designer:
   TANNY SHERBA
Architectural Consultant:
   LYNCH MARTINEZ

Project Architect:
   MICHAEL MUNDELL
Lighting Consultant:
   LIGHTING DESIGN
   COLLABORATIVE
Photographer:
   BARRY HALKIN

The 7400 sq. ft., state-of-the-art sports store includes a two lane running track, a tree house for camping gear, and a lined turf football field with a stadium ceiling. Other customer activities are a Gold Master Analyzer to test golf strokes, games like Fooz-Ball, Pop-a-Shot, darts and several video screens that feature sporting events. The mall shoppers are greeted by soft sculptures on bleachers seen through a racquetball glass storefront that is framed with statium-like columns. This store is not only customer oriented — it is customer participative.

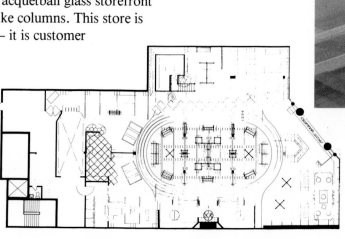

NIKE

W. Hollywood, CA

Design:
  PHH WALKER
  LOS ANGELES, CA
Principal-in-Charge:
  CLAIRE THOMSON
  PROJECT MANAGER
Project Designers:
  GORDON THOMPSON
  FRIEDA PANGESTU
Project Architect:
  GARY POPENOL
Nike Project Manager:
  PAUL MAGUIRE

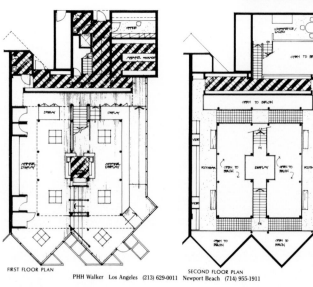

FIRST FLOOR PLAN

SECOND FLOOR PLAN

PHH Walker Los Angeles (213) 629-0011 Newport Beach (714) 955-1911

The interior space of 4300 sq. ft., with a very high ceiling and unusual glass exposure, was divided into a prototype for Nike retail stores where the customers could "experience" something special. The designers' approached the store layout from the point of view of the product; — building back lit galleries to showcase Nike's new line of neon-touched sports shoes and also providing space for the display and storage of apparel as well as shoes. The floor plan that evolved leads the consumer through the width, depth and height of the space, — to each merchandising center in the store. An interior stairwell was strategically placed in maximize those centers and also permit viewing from all levels. The materials that were selected represent the product; from the polished wood gym floor, — to the steel mesh that appears on the central stairway and on the floor as fixtures, — to glass blocks.

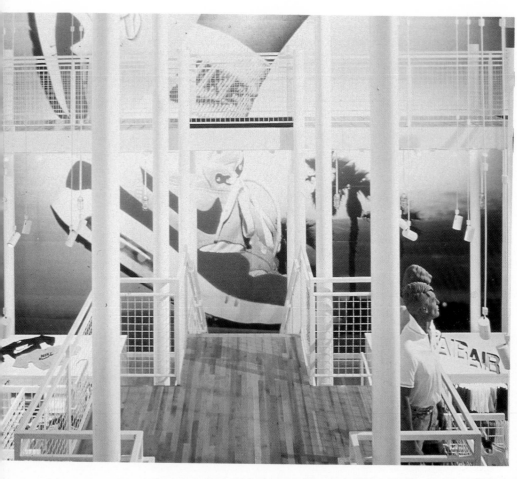

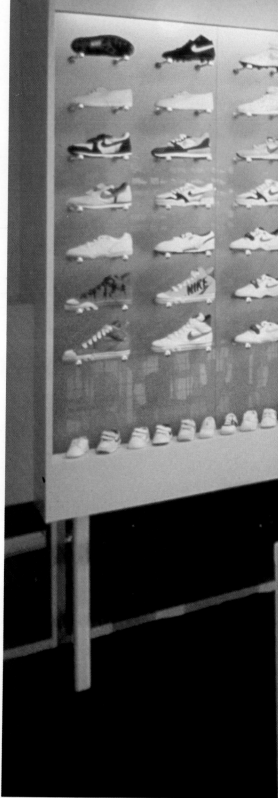

The 25' by 25' wall mural as seen from the upper, gallery level. The mural creates a strong image that penetrates through the entire vertical selling space. The same mezzanine level that was seen on the previous page, unfurnished, is seen here in the foreground completed with mannequin displays and selling fixtures. Two glass block "walkways" connect the two sides of the gallery level and thus make a "running track" where shoppers can test the product. One of these walkways is visible at the top of the photo.

Right: The "Shoe Art" gallery wall. The wall is backlit and the shoes are held in position on plexiglass platforms. To complete the gallery, there are graphics panels and TV monitors to play an in-store, taped visual message. There is a sense of excitement generated in the open space and the shopper is sure to remember the "shopping experience" at Nike.

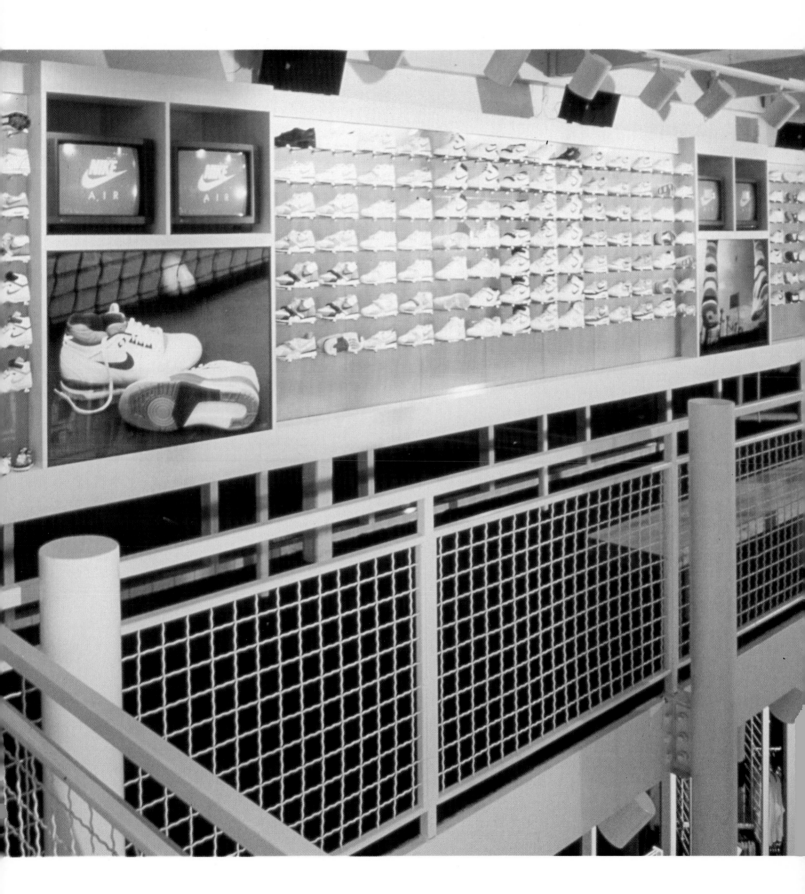

GYMEES

Twelve Oaks Mall, Novi, Michigan

Design:
JON GREENBERG ASSOCIATES,
BERKLEY, MI
Design Team:
KEN NISCH
JENNERS ANDERSON

The Gymees concept was developed by GNC, one of the nation's largest distributors of retail health foods. This store is their vehicle to market exercise equipment, activewear and workout fashions and vitamins. The storefront is sprayed with a synthetic material (Synaflex) to create the "concrete" texture, and the signature trademark mannequin (from Goldsmith) is split in half and applied to both sides of the glass. The "concrete" look of the store's floor is imported vinyl tile from Japan and red rubber tiles are used where the exercise machinery is located. Throughout, large poster graphics of muscular men and women make a visual appeal to today's health and body conscious consumers.

HOME FITNESS STUDIO

Short Hills Mall, Short Hills, NJ

Design:
SPARKS + CO.,
WESTCHESTER, IL
Fixture Contractor:
VERA CONSTRUCTION,
BRYSON, TX
Lighting:
HALO LIGHTING,
ELK GROVE VILLAGE, IL
Photographer:
JIM NORRIS, CHICAGO

Ninety lineal feet of glass wraps around most of the 2200 sq. ft. of this irregular shaped store in a very up-scaled mall. It is a prototype for stores that will show-case and demonstrate high quality exercise equipment while providing sales associates with a supportive environment for fitness counseling and be responsive to the customer's need for information. The designer came up with a "feature zone" concept. The zone is comprised of vertical stanchions upon which graphic panels can be mounted, and capped with a perforated metal canopy, and the unit will not only define the zone but the cap will also carry accent light for the products assembled below and the graphics on view. The store has been divided into a collection of "zones" where various merchandise is presented — and explained.

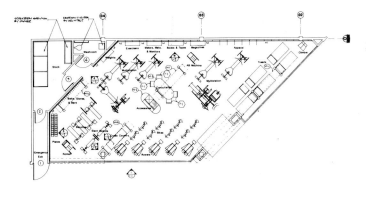

IMPULSE

New York, NY

Design:
    ALKER GROUP / CNI, NY
Project Executive:
    BILL KEENAN
Project Designer:
    JEAN LUGRIN
Project Coordinator:
    KENNETH SAN FELIPPO
Senior Graphic Designer:
    PETER SCAVUZZO

This is Circuit City's first entry into a mall under its new name, — Impulse. The store's appeal is to those interested and fascinated by things electronic, and the design and layout of the space emphasizes what makes Impulse unique; sales, service, stock and customer satisfaction. Positioned in the center core and visible immediately upon entry, high margin, advanced consumer electronics attract the impulse buyers. The

graphic elements and organized fixturing lead the shopper through the whole merchandise assortment. The interior is neutral gray and speckled in texture so that the graphics and products stand out under the controlled lighting in the ceiling. The grid of TV screens featured in the boxed off facade is repeated on the rear wall, under the high-tech framework that outlines the rear end of the store.

THE VIDEO STORE

Alliance Dr., Cincinnati, OH

Design:
RICHARDSONSMITH
Worthington, OH
Designers:
JODIE OLDS TURNER
ELLI GERDEMAN

Graphic Designer:
CHRIS PRATER
Strategic Merchandiser:
BETH DORSEY

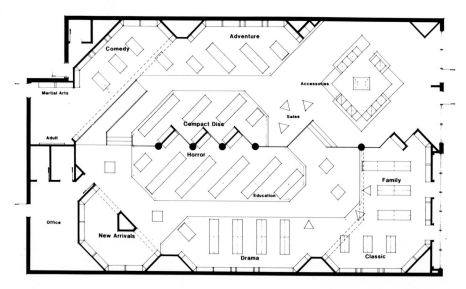

The 5000 sq. ft. prototype store was designed to encourage the shopper to move to all parts of the store, and to present to the shopper highlight themes, new releases and various categories as specific statements. An interior graphic communication system was devised to help the customer identify and locate the desired department, and general merchandise fixtures, as well as special feature fixtures, were created for maximum layout flexibility and unit capacity. Wall and floor high-capacity units have metal display panels with triangular shaped perforations which create a strong geometric pattern. A neutral background color was used generally and high chrome colors were used to feature and separate categories.

PERL PHOTO ELECTRONICS

World Finance Center, Winter Garden, NY

Design:
  ZB INC., NY
Principals:
  FREDERIC M. ZONSIUS &
  LORI A. BEITLER
Photographer:
  MAX HILAIRE

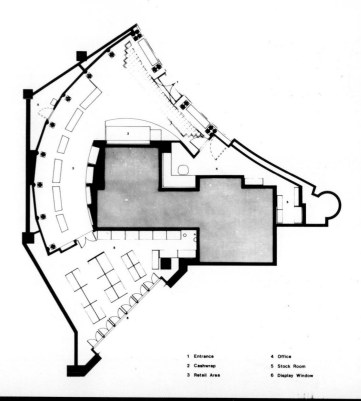

1	Entrance	4	Office
2	Cashwrap	5	Stock Room
3	Retail Area	6	Display Window

Viewed through the glass front, the store appears to be a wide sweep, — curving into infinity. Once inside the cool gray interior, the shopper is swept up by the arc of the counter, up front, and then carried along by the opposite curve, — to the rear of the shop. Along the way, "spoke-like" beams on the ceiling radiate out from the center core and join up with white vertical piers that separate the arced wall into individual shops or spheres of merchandise. The laminated fixtures with their angled glass fronts seem to lean forward — out into the general flow on the gray floor.

214

T.W. BEST

Northwestern Atrium Center, Chicago, IL

Design:
    EVA MADDOX ASSOCIATES,
    EVA MADDOX, PRES.
Designer:
    MARY BETH RAMPOLLA

Project Manager:
    J.D. MC KIBBEN
V.P. in Charge:
    PATRICK GRZYBEK

Photographer:
    JON WILLER
    HEDRICH BLESSING

Using bright colors and simple geometric shapes, the designers fashioned this award-winning prototype for their client. The concept was to take the traditional newsstand and turn it into a "new force in retailing." Within the 1100 sq. ft. space, the retailer can now accommodate a great volume of shoppers, and the angled placement of the main candy display draws the customers into the store and separates traffic and product zones. Ceiling banners and beam elements visually articulate the pathways from each entrance and "focus displays" allow for a high density of featured product to be shown within the architectural framework of the colorful store.

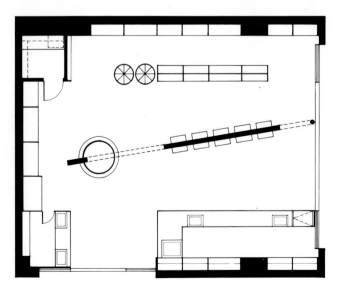

HENRY'S

Citicorp Building, San Francisco, CA

Design:
    PLANNING & DESIGN
    CONCEPTS, SAN FRANCISCO
Planner:
    STEWART WYLER
Designers:
    STEWART WYLER
    PETER MC CORMICK
Photographer:
    DOUG SALIN, SAN FRANCISCO

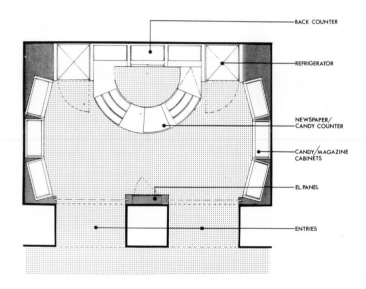

Located in the luxurious marbled lobby of an historically preserved building, is this handsome, "traditional," convenience store/newsstand. The central counter, in the 11' by 17' space, is curved to maximize the usable space and the counter is set in counterpoint to the curved side walls. The concave and convex forms provide easy access from the dual entrances to the merchandise — and set up the traffic flow. The products are highlighted by low-voltage spots built into the overhead storage areas. The curvilinear design and the selection of dark woods, marble and brass "combine an old world, traditional ambience with modern convenience shopping."

218

CHIASSO

Madison St., Chicago, IL

Design:
FLORIAN/WIERZBOWSKI
Partners:
PAUL FLORIAN
STEPHEN WIERZBOWSKI
WILLIAM WORN
Project Architect:
BERNADETTE PLANERT

Graphic Design:
R. VALICENTI/THIRST
Lighting Consultant:
CHICAGO LIGHTING
Stylist:
PEG VASILAK / STYLE
Photographer:
WAYNE CABLE /
CABLE STUDIO

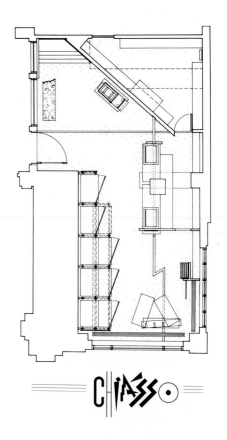

Entered through a lobby in a busy downtown commercial building, Chiasso is a 870 sq. ft. store that sells "up beat and off the beat" housewares, furniture, gifts and games — for home and office. The name, in Italian, means "uproar" or "sensation" and the owner, Kevin Wilder of Wilder Designs, selected it to express the playful and outrageous attitude of the very contemporary merchandise collected in the shop. That attitude had to be expressed in the store's look. "The design is a stage set which romanticizes the process and materials of the 20th cent. construction. It is at once analytical and nostalgic." Thus, the new materials that are used in the execution of the design are "synthetic versions of corporate office materials and the elements that existed are altered to look synthetic — in the tradition of synthetic cubism."

Right: A look into the store and the display window in the rear. On the left, the cash/wrap desk and on the right wall, — a pipe construction that holds many small items.

Above: The pipe assemblage that serves as a fixture system and also provides some of that 20th cent. look to the shop. *On the left:* A view of the cash/wrap which is centrally located for visibility and security, also the displayers the shopper sees upon entering the shop from the lobby. The stripes on the floor refer back to the first Chiasso shop (still thriving on Oak St.) and they also serve as directionals into and around the compact space. Faux granite, faux brushed aluminum, faux ebonized oak, faux paint textured laminates and bronze emphasize "the interaction and movement of forms" of the cash/wrap desk. The ductwork above and existing wall surfaces are textured to affect a uniform background for the merchandise. The "incomplete scaffolding" (above) supports dislocated fragments of table tops sheathed in faux granite and faux pigskin laminates, and the lowered exposed lighting restates the stage-set character of this fun-faux design.

SAMUEL PEPYS

1st Canadian Pl., Toronto, Ont., Canada

Design:
    THE INTERNATIONAL
    DESIGN GROUP, TORONTO
Executive V.P.:
    R. MAC LACHLIN
Architect/Designer:
    NELLA FIORINO &
    PAULIS CISKEVICIUS

The client wanted a traditional environment to show off the modern day products; small, beautiful and functional items of stationery. The appeal was to be to the "high profile customer" — a person of taste and sophistication and the ability to pay for something better. The space is only 250 sq. ft., but it is a well chosen space in a high traffic corridor of an office building with a natural skylight in it. Thus, they created a Beidermeier inspired bibliteque to honor the 17th century diarist whose name fronts the store. The totally glazed facade literally disappears and the viewer sees the fixtures which have been laid out in a repetitive format. Classic Beidermeier details are incorporated in the design of the inlayed burlwood and cherry veneer cases and fixtures and black lacquered columns, and fittings are used to accent and "authenticate" the look.

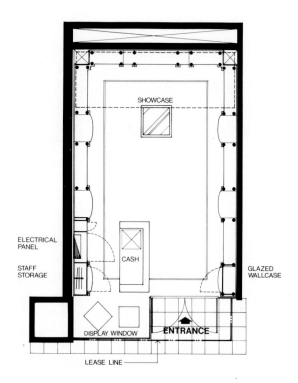

DEPARTMENT STORES

Today's department store is more than just shops-within-the-shop. It is more than just designer boutiques and brand name shops strung up along a wide marble aisle under a floating, multi-leveled ceiling washed with soft light. The department store has become a Yuppie Bazaar, an up-scaled theatrical event, — a space filled with color and light, and throbbing with the excitement of new things being presented in even newer ways. Today's store is designed to combat the ennui of ho-hum shoppers, and to instill in them the idea that this is the place to be — cause this is where "it" is happening. It is not being done with pyrotechnics, sharp colors, tooth-tingling and nerve-rattling clashes of textures and lighting techniques. It is being done with suave sophistication, — with a sense of style — sometimes with tradition — with rich materials and warm ambiences. The new department stores are designed to stroke, to pamper, to soothe and succor the shopper; make him/her stay longer and shop more. Restaurants and cafes are located within the store as are the amenities that make that longer stay possible. The dressing rooms are image-building spaces with lighting that flatters the shopper and enhances the outfit. Good traffic patterns, visual focal points, ceilings that intrigue as well as direct and add intimacy, the fixtures that come up to the aisle to show off what is new; all contribute to taking the ordeal out of shopping and cater to the individual who wants to shop — unhurried and unharried, but with an effective use of her time.

Minimalism is out and elegance is in. Away with the spare and the sparse, the naked and the unadorned. In with the details, the decoratives, — the rich materials and sumptuous textures. Many of the "isms" and "istics" of the '70s are out and we seem to be turning to the Classics, — Neo and not so Neo. Architectural firms that specialize in department store design are stressing this return to refinement, — to quiet elegance and the adaptation of bygone design elements that immediately suggest to the shopper a sense of status, class — and security. Edward Hambrecht of Hambrecht Terrell International, the company is represented in this chapter by the new Bloomingdales in Chicago, at a State of Retail Design presentation spoke of the "grandeur and permanent architectural features" that have returned to retail design. More elegant and luxurious materials are being employed. In the '50s and '60s, the emphasis was on function, but today's store must create a permanent architectural framework within which Visual Merchandising and Display will "become the area of dynamic and constant change" within the store.

Charles Sparks, also of HTI, in his presentation stressed, "the best stores express the times," and they satisfy the customers who are increasingly more sophisticated and demand better quality products, services and places to shop. "The challenge for retail designers is to invigorate store design and discover 'hot signals' in materials, products, colors and human services."

We are now reaching back to historical references because many customers, — especially the older and more affluent ones, are more comfortable with the past. With this backwards stretch, — we are reaching into the future. These retail establishments will probably still be fresh and fashionable in ten years from now as they sail into the next century, — looking good. Our selections are filled with the sights, sounds, and even smells that make up the "pleasure quotient" in Retailing — and with that pleasure in mind, — the chapter follows.

Left: The Bon Marche, Bellevue, WA.

THE BON MARCHE

Bellevue Square, Bellevue, WA

Building Architect:
WILLIAM POLK ASSOC.
SEATTLE, WA

Lighting Consultant:
THE KONDOS LIGHTING
CONSULTANT, NY

Floor Fixtures:
STORE KRAFT MNFG.
BEATRICE, NE

Perimeter Fixtures:
TOM BODEN STORE
FIXTURES, PORTLAND, OR

For Bon Marche:
RON SPENCER, SVM,
V.P. DIRECTOR OF V.M.

Photographer:
ELLIOT FINE

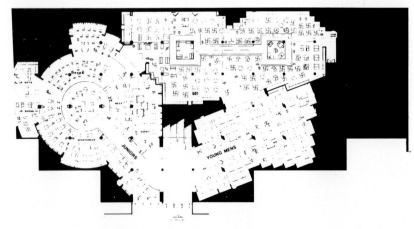

The Cube and Tiger shop won top awards in the recent NRMA/ISP store design contest in the department store category. Targeted at the young customer, — the Junior or Young Man, — the area consists of specialty stores on the lower level of the department store. The ceramic tile patterns, on the floor, are coordinated with the ceiling designs. In Junior, the ceiling cove is washed with multi-bands of traveling neon lights which move from the entrance of the store into the core of the department.

All free standing and perimeter wall fixtures were custom designed. Many fixtures have a charcoal, hammer-tone finish, — as do the metal grid systems used throughout. Selected walls and the fitting rooms were painted with zolatone but most of the walls were painted with "veiling lacquer," — a multi-coated, custom finish with a gloss white background and a large, textured, black string spatter over the white. The

Young Men's area (*right*) is accented with high gloss lacquered fin walls with bull nose edges. The field porcelain tiled floor is light gray and matte finished, while the aisle is polished light gray textures with matte and edged with a gloss granite border. Overhead, zigging and zagging in step with the floor pattern, are bands of neon light. In the subdued setting, the high-lighting spots seem even more effective.

A different Bon Marche and an adaptation of the Cube and Tiger shop, in the store in Bellingham, WA. The focal point of this design is the dome-shaped ceiling cove "runway," 6' by 45' long, that is accented by an everchanging flow of rainbow colored neon. This computerized painting with light creates an energized activity level that is the equivalent of the life-styles of the Junior customers, — and the merchandise. The planning direction was established on a "donut aisle" layout, and the center of the "donut" (*left*) was the hub or focal point of the whole floor. The center is outlined in black, and on the charcoal platform the mannequins stage an ever-changing fashion show. *Below:* The start of the ceiling runway that leads to the central hub. Along the way, metal grid panels on floor to ceiling black tubular supports carry the names of the specialty areas and serve as backgrounds for the displays off the aisle.

PARISIAN Hamilton Pl. Mall, Chattanooga, TN

Principal in Charge:
    ROBERT W. SCHAFER
Project Planner:
    DALE PAYTON

Project Designer:
    BARRY VINYARD
Parisian's Dir. of Store Planning:
    C. CAMPBELL

Parisian's Dir. of Design:
    J. MITCHELL
Photographer:
    JIM NORRIS

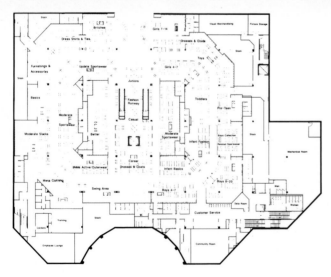

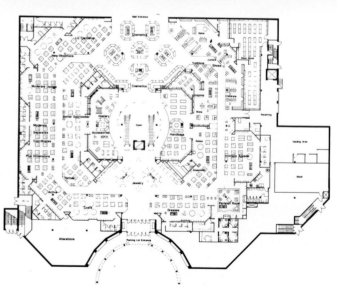

The 92,000 sq. ft. Parisian specialty department store is entered through a dominating exterior entrance that was designed to integrate with the store's interior. The large radius entrance is echoed by the mall entrance, a 15' high opening with a sweeping vaulted ceiling. The threshold from the mall to the store is reduced so that the shopper is actually 30' into the Parisian before becoming aware of the change of venue. The entrance from the lower level of the mall is treated in a similar design style. Once inside, high ceilings lead the shopper to the round escalator well opening where vertical transportation is provided. A skylight and clock tower add to the theatrics of the core area. Juniors is located at the bottom of the well, and serves to connect the upper level Women's Fashions with those located on the lower level along with Men's, Children's and Junior wear. Neon and wire grids bridge the gap between Men's and Young Men's which is viewed from the entrance and expresses an "aggressive attitude." Throughout the store, unique materials are employed like faceted ceramic tiles in alternating colors, leather floor tiles for the elegant Parisian Room, uniweb industrial wall coverings in Junior Shoes, also black, back-painted panels, corrugated metal, etched glass and faux marble.

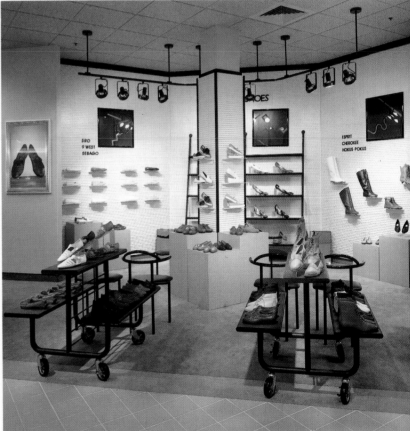

Left: At the base of the well, — the Junior area with its high-tech fixtures and surfacing materials. The lighting is integrated into the incline of the escalator as well as the ceiling. Black accent tubes surround the space and provide support for the focusable spots that highlight the merchandise on display.

DUTY FREE SHOP Chinachen, Hong Kong

Design:
TSL DESIGN GROUP,
LOS ANGELES, CA

Principals:
TAK TODA
RICHARD LEWIS,
TSUYOSHI SUGAUCHI

Last spring marked the opening date of the largest of the 150 Duty Free Shops with this "specialty department store" in Chinacin, Hong Kong. The 72,000 sq. ft. flagship is a two storey building and it is entered through the rear bus drop-off where shoppers are easily directed up the escalator and through the ten different departments. The flooring materials and the carpeting outline the flow in and around the various retail pathways and sections. After shopping the five departments on the upper level, a second escalator (shown here) descends to the lower level, and the balance of the departments and the exit.

Imported materials are used to create specific environments and add to the total interior design of the store. Circulation from area to area is defined by light and dark, — by the colors and values of the rich materials that are used throughout. Rhythm from one space to the next is delineated by Italian marble and tile floors and custom carpets. Hard flooring in the aisle direct traffic towards soft, comfortable "rooms" which are furnished with tables and pieces imported from Italy. American made ready-to-wear fixtures are enhanced with Canadian crown moldings, — to add to the cosmopolitan look of the store. Rusted metals,

patina finishes and high gloss lacquers also contribute to the high style of the design. Further architectural enhancements are the ornamental elements such as the large etched glass work in the escalator/lobby areas, and the museum quality wood sculptures and full scale Chinese figure replicas that add so much to the store's ambience, and also helps establish the store's sense of "place." "Specific lighting solutions, color selection and visual merchandising play equally strong roles in each separate department." The graphics and signage add to the corporate and environmental image of this award winning store.

BLOOMINGDALE'S

900 North Michigan, Chicago, IL

Design:
    HAMBRECHT TERRELL
    INTERNATIONAL, NY
President & Creative Director:
    JAMES TERRELL
Principal-in-Charge:
    ROBERT J. CERRETTI &
    HARVE OESLANDER

Planner:
    MICHAEL KERN
V.P./Creative Principal:
    DEBRA M. ROBUSTO
Project Director:
    WILL PERERA
Project Architect:
    MARIO BARONE

Designers:
    GUNJI TACHIKAWA
    STEVE DUFFY
    BRYAN GAILEY
Project Coordinator:
    AUSMA ZEIDLICKIS
Architect Principals:
    DANIEL J. BARTELUCE &
    STEVE VENTO
For Bloomingdale's:
    JOE FECZKO, SVM, V.P. OF
    VISUAL MERCHANDISING
Photographer:
    THE SADIN GROUP

The dominant attraction of the new atrium mall on North Michigan Ave. in the new Bloomingdale's, — 250,000 sq. ft. of space that incorporates six selling floors and one for offices. *Left:* A view of the mall entrances on to the six selling levels as viewed from the largest escalator well in Chicago; 45' wide by 115' long and 108' high. The main floor of the store (below) is styled after Frank Lloyd Wright's Unity Temple in Oak Park and the Imperial Hotel in Tokyo. The free-standing columns are topped with mitred cornices and crown mouldings. The recessed wall panels and the etched glass panels reflect the Prairie School of architecture and styling. Maple wood is used on this level and the fine jewelry area is distinguished with polished hairwood. "Frank Lloyd Wright and the Prairie School evoke the broad sweeping vistas of Chicago. We drew on this influence to build a unique environment that reflects Bloomingdale's sense of drama and excitement, and the vitality of Chicago," said James Terrell of HTI.

The second level is mainly devoted to Men's wear, and here the designers found inspiration in Wright's Arizona Biltmore. Flying buttresses cantilever over the central aisle, and the backlit ceiling panels, wall lights and flooring patterns all feature right angle insets that reflect Wright's window pattern designs. The marble floor is mainly Anita Rosada marble from Spain, patterned in Ancona gray from Italy and Tanaga marble from the U.S. The "Boardroom," where men's fragrances are sold, features a moving L.E.D. screen that displays current stock prices, during the week, and sport's scores on the weekends. Off to one side is Saturday's Generation (above) where casual wear is set in a construction of industrial pipe framing and walkways for the mannequins. In this high-tech contemporary area, the relaxed fashions are deftly presented.

Above: The third level is styled after the Wright homes in suburban Oak Park. The marble aisles are a combination of Gail Premier and Teton, both American marbles. Greige oak, natural and ebonized Maple, and polished Mahogany woods are used on this level for wall detailing and cases. Women's wear, Children's wear, and specialty shops are located on Three.

Right: The fourth level is faithfully fashioned after the Boulevard on Four in the N.Y.C. store with its promenade of repeating columns that reach up to vaulted and domed ceilings. There are display platforms at the aisle intersections, and the dual toned granite creates directing patterns on the floors of the Promenade. The textured walls and striking architectural columns are finished in high impact, Imron paint. Also on Four is the shoe salon with its warm peach carpeting and walls, and display cabinets of blackened and pickled ash. A raised, vaulted ceiling glows with light and floats over the shop.

Below: Home Fashions is located on Five, and this level is fashioned after Wright's Falling Water house in Philadelphia. This level features suspended, backlit ceiling lights with inset, right angle details. Creamy Tempa marble from Portugal covers the aisles and natural and ebonized maple is used for the fixtures, cases and column enclosures.

Right: The Sixth floor — and The Main Course, — all with a strong bow to Wright's Robie House in Oak Park. The central concourse features arched ceilings, cross inset wall panels, and etched glass. Prairie School styling is updated with green neon tubing which accentuates the ziggurat displays. Much of the floor is covered with Vetro Grigio ceramic tile which contains inset chips of ground green glass to pick up the green neon that accents the level. In China and Glass, natural and ebonized Maple woods and gray hairwood are used for the floor and wall fixtures. "With this store, Bloomingdale's is at the head of two important retailing trends: The return to permanent architecture and a renewed commitment to urban centers as important retail markets," according to James Terrell.

MODERN STONE AGE, LTD.

Greene St., Soho, NY

Design:
   JEAN JACQUES FERRON &
   FRANCOIS VALLEE

In a century old, Cast Iron landmarked building, in artistic Soho, is this new entry in home fashion accessories. Using materials as old as the earth itself and a style-awareness as new as the next century, the shop is a blend of ancient and extremely new, — in a soothing, gray ambience. The walls channel the shopper into the store and lead to the dual level "space deck" at the rear. A spiral staircase rises to the office in the mezzanine. Sheets of marble are embedded in concrete for the flooring, and the walls are artfully textured and painted in grays and mauves. The owners/designers have assembled outstanding pieces by noted architects like Ettore Sottsass, Michele De Lucchi, and Giulio Lazzotti. Each design employs technology to enhance the natural beauty and character of the stone or marble, cement, metal or shells, — and many express a welcome sense of humor in the design. Artists and sculptors are also represented with "living sculptures" — functional pieces of art that have elements of permanence and timelessness, even though they are clocks, lamps, tables and wall pieces. Since the natural shapes and textures of the materials are so important in the products on display, the lighting creates deep shadows and some highlights in an otherwise low-keyed environment.

ABOUT THE EDITOR

Martin M. Pegler has long been considered a leading authority on store design and visual merchandising. He has been involved in the field for almost forty years and has worked in all phrases of Merchandise Presentation: designer, manufacturer, displayperson, store planner and consultant. Witty, urbane, erudite and most persuasive, he has long been a vocal champion of store design and visual presentation as a necessary and respected part of Retailing. This has made him a popular speaker across the country and for two tours of the British Isles, Mexico and Japan. He is in demand as a lecturer for industry, small business groups as well as, nation-wide chains and shopping centers.

Mr. Pegler is the author of numerous books on visual presentation and architecture. He is currently a professor of Store Planning and Visual Merchandising at the Fashion Institute of Technology in N.Y. and travels extensively, — always searching the field for new and fresh approaches, ideas and techniques to share.